PT
343
.M28

FINCH

Date Due		
FEB - 1 1983		
OCT 11 1994		

FINCH

172

LAST ESSAYS

By Thomas Mann

Winner of the Nobel Prize for Literature, 1929

FICTION

Confessions of Felix Krull, Confidence Man (1955)
The Black Swan (1954)
The Holy Sinner (1951)
Doctor Faustus (1948)
The Tables of the Law (1945)
The Transposed Heads (1941)
The Beloved Returns (1940)
Stories of Three Decades (1936)
Joseph and His Brothers (1933–1944)

1 THE TALES OF JACOB	3 JOSEPH IN EGYPT
2 YOUNG JOSEPH	4 JOSEPH THE PROVIDER

The Magic Mountain (1927)
Death in Venice (1925)
Buddenbrooks (1924)
Royal Highness (1916)

NON FICTION

The Story of a Novel (1961)
A Sketch of My Life (1960)
Last Essays (1959)
Essays of Three Decades (1947)
Listen, Germany! (1943)
Order of the Day (1942), *which included* THIS WAR (1940), THE COMING VICTORY OF DEMOCRACY (1938), THIS PEACE (1938), *and* AN EXCHANGE OF LETTERS (1937)
Freud, Goethe, Wagner (1937)
Three Essays (1929): FREDERICK AND THE GREAT COALITION; GOETHE AND TOLSTOI; AN EXPERIENCE IN THE OCCULT

Dates are those of the first American editions.

Alfred A Knopf, Publisher, New York

THOMAS MANN AT EIGHTY

JUNE 1955

Thomas Mann

LAST ESSAYS

TRANSLATED FROM THE GERMAN BY
Richard and Clara Winston

AND

Tania and James Stern

Alfred A. Knopf *New York*
1966

L. C. CATALOG CARD NUMBER: 59–5436

© ALFRED A. KNOPF, INC., 1958

THIS IS A BORZOI BOOK,
PUBLISHED BY ALFRED A. KNOPF, INC.

PUBLISHED FEBRUARY 16, 1959
SECOND PRINTING, OCTOBER 1966

The quotation on page 82 is reprinted with the permission of Oxford University Press, Inc., from Goethe's Faust, translated by Louis MacNeice.

CONTENTS

A NOTE ON THE VERSE TRANSLATIONS

THE translations of verse in the essays on Schiller and Goethe are intended to be utilitarian rather than beautiful. Translation of poetry is a sad enterprise at best, and the difficulty is compounded in the case of Schiller because his philosophical verse is often scarcely poetic to modern feeling; in the case of Goethe because his lyricism is so far superior to our modest talents. Yet rhyme and meter do convey a sense of the originals which would be entirely lost in a prose rendering. We have therefore attempted verse translations throughout, wherever nineteenth-century versions by Coleridge and Bulwer-Lytton were altogether inadequate. Where possible, we have borrowed from these translators, in some instances amending their lines to make them conform more closely to the German text as cited by Thomas Mann. The translations from Schiller's *Wallenstein* and *Don Carlos* are largely by Coleridge.

RICHARD AND CLARA WINSTON

LAST ESSAYS

ON SCHILLER

For the 150th anniversary of the poet's death.
Affectionately dedicated to his memory.

Am Himmel ist geschäftige Bewegung,
Des Turmes Fahne jagt der Wind, schnell geht
Der Wolken Zug, die Mondessichel wankt,
Und durch die Nacht zuckt ungewisse Helle.
Kein Sternbild ist zu sehen.

> The sky is fuming with a restless motion,
> The flag upon the tower lashed by wind;
> The clouds parade apace; the crescent moon
> Wavers, and misty flashes flicker through
> The night. No star's in sight.

SUCH was the night—that May night one hundred and fifty years ago when Friedrich Schiller's mortal remains were carried through the slumbering, deserted streets of Weimar from the Esplanade across the market square and down Jakobsgasse to the ancient graveyard of St. James's Church. No "fearful midnight tolling" added low sonorities to the sad scene. The bells were silent; silent the Bell whose song he had celebrated in a poem embracing the span of human life; no mourning peal accompanied this wanderer upon his last journey. There were no sounds but the dragging footsteps of the men, who now and then laid down their burden, the bier with the cheap, rough coffin on it, to rest and exchange places.

Actually, paid artisans should have been the pallbearers,

for that was the custom. It was the turn of the tailors' guild to draw the profit from this business. But at the last moment one sensitive man, long an ardent admirer of the poet, had protested against the indignity of committing the task to ignorant, unfeeling strangers. This man, Secretary Schwabe, had hastily recruited a group drawn from the intellectual professions—gentlemen with academic titles, men of law, and a sprinkling of artists, to form a solemn escort for the departed. Curiously enough, the theater was not represented. There were some twenty men in all; eight at a time took turns as pallbearers, while the others formed the procession. These were the only mourners.

They reached the old graveyard. Abutting the wall to the right of the gateway stood the Treasury Vault, a small, gray, ancient, windowless structure with a peaked black roof. An iron grill closed its entrance, while a trapdoor led into its dark crypt. The building bore this name because it belonged to the Treasury Board of the district.

Here the gravedigger and his assistants came forward and took charge of the coffin. The moon, emerging from the speeding clouds and almost immediately retreating into them again, for a moment cast a glow upon the plain wooden box. In the trees and in the rafters of the near-by church the wind puffed and soughed.

Probably the academic gentlemen followed the gravediggers to the vault, or as many of them as could stand in the limited space around the trapdoor. The rusty hinges squealed dismally as the door was pulled up. The coffin was slung in ropes and let down into the depths until it reached bottom—any bottom, among other coffins or upon them. Above the moldering night into which that plain box had vanished, the trapdoor closed. The hour was midnight, the midnight of the third day after Schiller's passing.

Did everyone remain for a few minutes with bared heads, in silent prayer, before taking leave? I imagine so. There was, at any rate, no more than this to the funeral; no strains of music; no words from the lips of priest or friends; no myrtle and laurels. We read that these unceremonious proceedings were customary in Weimar at the time. The Church service, the collect for the dead, was not held until the day after burial.

The collect on the afternoon of May 12 was marked by no special solemnity, since neither the Duke of Weimar nor Goethe was present. Goethe was ill, and news of his friend's death was probably withheld from him for a full day. Moreover, the widow, the family, even the dying man himself are said to have requested a quiet and unostentatious funeral. As for the nocturnal hour, it is said that the condition of the body necessitated haste.

Be that as it may, the *place* of burial befitted the social standing of the deceased, Ducal Court Councillor von Schiller. Only the remains of high personages whose families owned no hereditary vault of their own, only members of Weimar society such as the Koppenfels, Ridels, Von Pfuhls, Von Egloffsteins, and the like, were admitted to the "Treasury Vault." But we may add that this aristocratic vault offered the ladies and gentlemen far worse quarters than any other spot of ground beneath the sod of the common graveyard. Schiller's distich on the "spirit with the reversed torch" might well have been inscribed above the entrance:

> *Lieblich sieht er zwar aus, mit seiner erloschenen Fackel;*
> *Aber, ihr Herren, der Tod ist so ästhetisch doch nicht.*

> How very charming he looks, bearing his flameless brand;
> Yet, my dear sirs, death is not so aesthetic as that.

Inside that dank cavern death worked in a particularly unaesthetic manner. Dampness oozed through walls and floors; the wood of the coffins lying higgledy-piggledy moldered rapidly; so that later, when a summary clearance of the vault was impending, pious posterity had the greatest difficulty picking a particular skull and the bones belonging to it from the chaotic mass of corruption. Indeed, in the case of Schiller the whole skeleton could never be recovered, nor could there be any certainty that the remains so rescued were those of the poet.

The mourners stood about, sighed, departed. Did they hear amid the rustling and groans of the wind a faint, sweet melody, the elfin voices of a disembodied choir hovering around the burial vault?

> *Nur der Körper eignet jenen Mächten,*
> *Die das dunkle Schicksal flechten;*
> *Aber frei von jeder Zeitgewalt,*
> *Die Gespielin seliger Naturen*
> *Wandelt oben in des Lichtes Fluren*
> *Göttlich unter Göttern die* Gestalt.

> The flesh alone is prey to those dark powers
> Ever weaving at our destinies;
> Freed of bondage to the hours,
> Playmate of blissful entities,
> The pure form rises to Elysian bowers,
> Itself divine among divinities.

That pure form had already risen. Transported beyond the ignominy of matter, wearing an aureole of manly ideality, of ideal manhood, bold, passionate, and gentle all at once, turning its princely countenance toward the stars with a savior's gaze, that pure form soared in the very hour of his burial. That immortal form was consigned at once to the close affection of his people, to the tender concern of all mankind. Upon his brow, ennobled by the "dignity of thought," glows (as, in the poem, it glows on the brow of the Titan) the double radiance of "sensual bliss and peace of soul"—expressive of the artist's idea that beauty frees us from the onerous choice between the two; that beauty produces a humanized union of sensuality and morality, reconciles our earthly and our higher beings, forms the bridge between reality and the ideal;

that the divergent images of "the good" in the aesthetic and moral worlds are fused in the artist's celebration of it. Beauty and truth merge in art, that educator of the human race.

We wish to pay homage to this beneficent spirit who has risen to Elysian bowers. How shall we do so? Who am I to speak in his praise, confronted as I am by mountains of learned appreciations and analyses which scholarship has reared in the past hundred and fifty years? In my diffidence I am emboldened by only one thing, and that of a rather naïve and simple-hearted nature. This is the kinship of experience, the brotherhood, the intimacy which exists among all creative artists, irrespective of stature, epoch, or character. As for Schiller, he was a spirit before which no artist need feel wholly timid and ill at ease, wholly unworthy. For that spirit was and remains the prototype of the artist. He paid tribute to art in acts of such splendor, in words of such eloquence, that even the least among his fellows can with modest pride recognize his own anguish and his own joy.

Wenn, das Tote bildend zu beseelen,
Mit dem Stoff sich zu vermählen,
Tatenvoll der Genius entbrennt,
Da, da spanne sich des Fleißes Nerve,
Und beharrlich ringend unterwerfe
Der Gedanke sich das Element.
Nur dem Ernst, den keine Mühe bleichet,
Rauscht der Wahrheit tief versteckter Born:
Nur des Meißels schwerem Schlag erweichet
Sich des Marmors sprödes Korn.
Aber dringt bis in der Schönheit Sphäre,
Und im Staube bleibt die Schwere
Mit dem Stoff, den sie beherrscht, zurück.
Nicht der Masse qualvoll abgerungen,
Schlank und leicht, wie aus dem Nichts gesprungen,
Steht das Bild vor dem entzückten Blick.

When the spirit kindles with desire
To shape dead matter, lend it life's own fire,
To take crude mass and pass it on refined—
It must be done by straining every nerve;
Only unflinching constancy will serve
To subjugate the elements to Mind.
For Truth in her mysterious deep spring
Yields only to the one who spares no pain,
As marble only can be made to sing
Under the chisel's merciless refrain.
But once the shape of beauty has been found
All weight lies with the chips upon the ground.
And from the massive block, now free to rise,
Slender and light, as it were made of air,
Showing no trace of all the pangs and care,
The statue stands before enraptured eyes.

How perfectly that is said. How cogently it voices, in language somewhat inflated but still precise, every artist's aims and experience. How, moreover, in a single glorious stanza of his poem *The Artists* he has hymned the intermediary powers of art, which brings the sublime within the ken of earthly mortals. With what gratitude he has extolled the magnanimity of the only one among the celestial beings who deigns to share man's lot: the goddess of Truth.

Die, eine Glorie von Orionen
Ums Angesicht, in hehrer Majestät,
Nur angeschaut von reineren Dämonen,
Verzehrend über Sternen geht,
Geflohn auf ihrem Sonnenthrone,
Die furchtbar herrliche Urania,
Mit abgelegter Feuerkrone
Steht sie—als Schönheit vor uns da.
Der Anmut Gürtel umgewunden,
Wird sie zum Kind, daß Kinder sie verstehn:

Was wir als Schönheit hier empfunden,
Wird einst als Wahrheit *uns entgegen gehn.*

Wearing Orion's glories on her brow,
Visible only to the good and great
—Pure spirits, who her majesty avow—
Urania sweeps above the starry spheres,
And with her flaming chaplet laid aside,
Upon her sun-illumined throne appears
—Beauty personified—our light and guide.
With every attribute of grace endued,
Her childlike innocence appeals to youth,
And that which is today as Beauty viewed
Anon will prove to be the very Truth.

And indeed, for all his deep earnestness, his unflagging thoughtfulness, and the keenness of his intellect, who can overlook the childlike element in Schiller's nature, the noble naïveté which so often elicits a smile from us? Yet our smile is one of respect and affection, for that simplicity is an inseparable part of his special and incomparable greatness. We must first and foremost perceive and bow to this innate, involuntary greatness to which not one of his ideas, not a single act of his mind, ever played false. Goethe, in his old age, never wearied of praising this aspect of Schiller's greatness. Recollecting that very innateness and involuntariness, the aged poet was perennially astonished. "Do what he would," Goethe said, "he could produce nothing that failed to surpass the best work of the moderns; in fact, when Schiller cut his fingernails, he was greater than these worthies."

I do not know why a work that was of minor importance to Schiller, and that is truly minor among his major works, has always appeared to me the most striking example of this instinctive greatness. I refer to *The Song of the Bell.* What do those ten or twelve pages of short, rhythmically alternating stanzas amount to compared with the brilliant major achievements of his life, the magnificent dramatic exploits such as

Wallenstein, William Tell, or the colossal *Demetrius?* The scoffing romantics could have a laugh at the old-fashioned homeliness of the poem. What is it, after all, but a description of a bell's casting, accompanied by "fine words"? Fine words about everything imaginable, about the whole pattern of human existence, as represented in the tolling of the bell; for "heartless itself, and without feeling," the bell rings out the "swift alternations of life," the prototypal, recurrent stations and events which are purified into *mythos.* The scoffers' mockery at a poem of this order was not only tasteless, it was an act of downright malice.

Yet undeniably there is a good deal of the comic in this evocation of normality and decent orderliness: the lines about the hard-working family man and the "prudent housewife," the passages such as "No more with girls content to play, Bounds the proud boy on his way," and "Blushing, he glides where'er she moves," and "When the nations free themselves, the commonwealth will thrive no more." Without being spiteful and captious, we may well ask who is going to free the nations if they do not do it themselves. But all this does not keep this poem from being the equal of anything the man ever addressed himself to, from being utterly expressive of his sovereign genius. Wilhelm von Humboldt's opinion remains just: "I know of no poem in any language which displays so wide a range in so small a compass, which runs the gamut of all the deepest human emotions, and in wholly lyrical fashion shows life as if in an epic enclosed within natural boundaries." And indeed Schiller's name has always been specially linked with this poem, in Germany and throughout the world. Enormous popularity came his way almost from the moment of its appearance, and has begun to vanish only now, in the shades of that night of ignorance and forgetfulness which is enfolding us. But it is not long since the simplest souls among the people knew the whole poem by heart. The same was true of the upper classes. The Danish writer Herman Bang comments in one of his *Eccentric Stories* on an actor at court: "He was the only person in the hall who was not quite sure of his lines in *The Bell.*"

It is not easy to stop, once I have begun to speak of Schiller's special greatness—a generous, lofty, flaming, inspiring grandeur such as we do not find even in Goethe's wiser, more natural and elementary majesty; a greatness both intoxicated with the universe and didactically humanistic, but always and above all supremely manly. And within this almost excessive, almost anti-natural manliness, alongside this espousal of will, freedom, awareness, there lurks the artist-child who sees nothing nobler in this world than *play;* who declares that man alone of all creatures knows how to play and is wholly man only when he plays. Granted, this is aesthetic philosophy. But the smile we occasionally have to suppress in the face of Schiller's grand tone is directed less toward the tone than toward an eternal boyishness which is part of it, toward his delight in an exalted game of cowboys and Indians, as it were. For he was prone to revel in adventure and psychological sensationalism, in antithetic biographies à la Plutarch, in terrible virtue and heroic criminality. His imagination was fired by the "unspeakable greatness" of stealing crowns, by eccentricity and unusual corruption, by reports of crimes, the history of remarkable conspiracies and rebellions, Jesuit intrigues, the Inquisition, the Bastille, or the perils of gambling.

His boyishness also is manifest in the insubstantiality of his female characters, his Amalias and Theklas—manifest, too, in the braggart lewdness with which he attempts to compensate for the pallor of such characters. Thus, he daringly makes Fiesco say: "A female is most beautiful in her nightgown—that is the costume of her trade." To which Julia Imperiali replies: "How frivolous!" Indeed it is inordinately frivolous! Moreover, did not this puerility, this eternal boyishness of his, continue far beyond the early stage of his creative life, from which *Fiesco* stems? Is it not also to be found in his mature art, in the often excessive exuberance of his rhetoric, in his highly contrived theatricality, product of a conspiracy between imagination and nature—and in his passion for heaping shock upon shock in his tragedies? Goethe refers to this last in a conversation with Eckermann. During the staging of his *Egmont*, he relates, Schiller kept urging him to change the prison scene in which Egmont hears his death sentence read. Schiller would have had Alba appear in the background, masked and enveloped in a cloak, to gloat over Egmont's terror of death. We must picture the two dissimilar friends, Goethe laughingly protesting: "No, no, my dear fellow—really, now, what are you thinking of? Why, that would be too gruesome!" And Schiller insisting: "But I swear to you, it will make a tremendous impression. The audience will simply swoon."

"He was a great, a strange man," Goethe said, with a sadly serene shake of his head, memories thronging to his mind. And, lost in thoughts of his friend as he so frequently was, he would recall instances of Schiller's typically Thespian indifference, even distaste for establishing motivation. His idea had been to have Gessler simply pluck an apple from a tree and order Tell to shoot it from his son's head. And, Goethe reminisced, what a time he had had prevailing on his friend to introduce at least a few verses in which the boy boasted of his father's ability to shoot an apple from a tree at a hundred paces, so that the tyrant might later seize upon this hint and stipulate the famous feat of marksmanship. Subsequently, Schiller sent these verses to Iffland with a letter saying that these were revisions he had made because he felt a certain lack of motivation in the original text. He did not mention that someone else had had to point out this cavalier negligence.

My mind still rests on that trait of eternal boyishness and adventurousness which is the curious complement to Schiller's sublimity. Like Balzac, he had a fantastic bent for planning grand business deals, which emerges especially in his correspondence with the publisher Cotta. Time and again in these letters he suggests vast, sprawling enterprises, considers various opportunities for speculations, weighs the chances for success and profits on a grand scale. It would appear that his speculative activity was not limited to philosophy; speculation in general was a passion with him. Yet his ardent soul could practice it on the highest plane of idealism, as is witnessed by his founding of the *Horen*. For this periodical he eloquently enlisted the co-operation of everyone of importance in intellectual Germany—Fichte, Dalberg, Herder, Hufeland, the two Humboldts, Matthisson, and no other than Privy Councillor von Goethe. His aim was nothing less than to create an organization of the intellectuals. How foreign was any such idea, any such altruistic aspiration, to the last-named of these associates. When Schiller occasionally voiced distress at Goethe's egoistic lethargy, he was referring to this cool indifference toward organization. Part and parcel of Schiller's worldly enthusiasms was the outgoing desire to influence cultural affairs, and to this end he was quite willing to exercise diplomacy, which was likewise not in Goethe's character. "Schiller," Goethe said, and the words sound surprising on the lips of this courtier and man of the world, "had far more worldly wisdom and manner than I, and considered far more carefully what he said than I did—for I often affrighted good people by rash utterances and spoiled the effectiveness of some of my best measures."

Is it any wonder, for that matter, that one who was rising from low estate, who had learned the lessons of want, and whose ambition had been spurred by indigence, who was eager to bestride the great place in the world to which his genius entitled him, should have developed more diplomacy than a fortune's darling born to proud estate who did not need to consider so carefully what he said? "When Schiller conquers kingdoms, he undoubtedly has had his eye on them all along," wrote Hermann Grimm, the keenest psychologist among the critics of Schiller.

The greatest kingdom Schiller conquered was Goethe's friendship. Could this have been won entirely without deliberation and diplomacy? Goethe, just back from Italy, was wary and reticent, felt himself "caught in a troublesome squeeze between Ardinghello and Franz Moor." It is said that he and Schiller chanced to depart together from a meeting of the Society for Natural Science in Jena. I cannot believe that this was altogether fortuitous, nor that by sheer chance Schiller opened the conversation with a remark which immediately electrified Goethe—so that the latter could not forbear to deliver an eloquent impromptu lecture on the matter dearest to his heart, the theory of the metamorphosis of plants, and by way of illustration to describe an archetypal plant, the *Urpflanze*. All this, be it noted, to the author of *The Robbers*, of that unpleasant drama *Don Carlos*, and of that virtually seditious essay on *Grace and Dignity*. And how did Schiller respond but with that famous remark: "Experience knows of no such plant; that is a mere concept, is it not?" This startling discourtesy might have put an end to the conversation; instead, it enlivened it. For when Goethe, stung, replied: "I am indeed glad to hear that I have concepts in my head without knowing it, and that they even take material shape before my eyes," Schiller immediately and adroitly shifted ground. For he had not at all intended to have the conversation broken off; he desired, as Goethe well knew, "to attract me more than repel me," if only on account of the *Horen*, since he hoped to have *Wilhelm Meister* for the periodical. Therefore he replied "as a cultivated Kantian," and the dispute continued happily for a long while in spite of all the contradictions between the two men—spiced, in fact, by these very contradictions. For, Goethe says, "Schiller had a great attractiveness; he captivated all who approached him" (or whom he approached). The upshot was that Goethe promised to contribute to the magazine. The ice was broken, and an antipodal friendship launched—the most famous of all intellectual alliances, which was to bear such rich fruit out of the reciprocal influence of two great spirits upon one another. But there can be no doubt that the friendship originated on Schiller's conscious initiative, that he cleverly maneuvered it. Given Goethe's lethargy in such matters and his initial wariness, the two men would have lived side by side without contact, had Schiller not laid his snares.

Psychology easily leads one to impiety. Yet lack of piety is simply one aspect, the naturalistic side, as it were, of truth. Hence I will be so blasphemous as to suggest that the noted birthday letter in which Schiller, "with the hand of friendship" and with unparalleled cleverness, drew up "the sum of Goethe's existence" was also in good part a work of diplomacy. At bottom, in fact, the same is true of the priceless treatise *On Naïve and Sentimental Poetry*, which suggests in its superlatively brilliant fashion that speculative and intuitive minds, given genius in both, must meet halfway, because they are of equal rank and belong together. In brief, this essay, too, was a cast to win a great place, the place at Goethe's side.

Am I right or wrong in saying that diplomacy, purposefulness, "going after" something, has about it something childlike in conjunction with a mind so great as Schiller's? Titles were bestowed upon him—and obviously the story is not complete when we say that he merely accepted these. He went after them. In 1784, at the age of twenty-five, he had occasion to read aloud to Duke Karl August of Weimar the first act of *Don Carlos*, then just completed. "Why, that is excellent," the Duke said. "Really?" Schiller replied. "Then would Your Highness be so gracious as to confer the title of Councillor upon me?" "Why, with the greatest pleasure!" Karl August laughed—and the rescript was quickly drawn up.

"Councillor" is good, but "Court Councillor" is still better.

This title, too, did not descend on Schiller out of the blue; he
acquired it in 1790, shortly before his marriage, by asking the
Duke of Meiningen for it. Twelve years later—in the mean-
time *Wallenstein, Mary Stuart,* and *The Maid of Orleans*
were behind him—it was again Karl August who applied to
the Emperor to have Germany's foremost dramatist raised
to the hereditary nobility—certainly not without that dramatist's urging. Thus he became, for the brief remainder of his
life, *Herr Hofrat von* Schiller. And how he loved his title,
though he must have known well in his big, child's heart that
this earthly pomp would fall away from him at the moment
of his passage to a better world, and that in his immortal
shape he would be Friedrich Schiller again, as he had been in
the days of his rebellious youth under the rod of a tyrant.

The child in the man, the child in the artist—lastly, cannot we find the glorious trait of eternal boyishness again in
the years of penance which this powerful artist imposed on
himself, the years of philosophical speculation, aesthetic
metaphysics, and criticism during which he sternly re-
nounced poetic creativity for the sake of freedom? For he
felt the dark, unconscious impulses of art to be compulsively
non-human, unworthy of man as a free, ethical being. He re-
solved not to surrender to creativity until he had raised in-
stinctuality to the level of clear, conscious, rational law. "It
was distressing," Goethe said, still troubled years afterward,
"to see so extraordinarily talented a person torment himself
with philosophical modes of thought which could not help
him at all." "Accursed" was the word Goethe used of that
period of speculative activity during which Schiller ear-
nestly endeavored to free sentimental poetry wholly from
naïve poetry, and found himself utterly unable, of course, to
find any sound foundation for the former—a tragic discovery which caused him unspeakable confusion. "As if," old
Goethe added, smiling, "sentimental poetry could exist at all
without a naïve basis from which it springs."

That is the smile of age's wisdom at a touching display of

childish obstinacy. Yet the stubborn child's creative powers triumphantly survived the moil and toil of philosophizing, passed through it and reached a higher plane of productivity in ennobled simplicity. About to embark on his *Wallenstein*, he wrote: "It is really only in art that I feel my powers; in theory I am prey to a thousand conflicting principles. There I am only a dilettante. . . . Criticism must now recompense me for the harm it has done me. And it has indeed harmed me, for I have now lacked for several years the boldness, the living fire I possessed before I knew a single rule. Nowadays I *see* myself creating and shaping; I observe the play of inspiration; and my imagination is fettered by awareness of an onlooker. But let artistic form once again become second nature to me, as learning is to an educated man, and imagination will recover her eternal freedom and know no limits but those she has set herself."

It is plain that he goes on speculating even as he attempts to send speculation packing. What he is counting upon is a second era of simplicity and unconsciousness—the miracle of resurrected naïveté. He did not miscalculate, and there is no need for us to deplore, along with Goethe, the five years sacrificed to theory and criticism; we may not say that they were useless to Schiller's mighty talent. At first, no doubt, those years set barriers in the way of that talent's emergence, rendered the poet more exacting, more fastidious, even more squeamish toward his own talent. But their net effect was to enable him to purify and ennoble his inspiration, which before, even in *Don Carlos*, had been a headlong and wild force. His art now showed true sovereignty instead of wanton exuberance. "This I have learned from working on this play," he wrote at the time he was in the midst of *The Maid of Orleans*, "one must never let oneself be bound by any fixed ideas of form. Rather, one must bravely invent a new form for each new subject, always allowing the subject to dictate the principles of genre."

• • •

This strikes a thoroughly practical note. It expresses a refreshingly realistic attitude toward form, toward art. In the light of it we feel more than ever that the nimbus of sky-blue idealism which has ringed him with a conventional halo has been of too pale a shade, that the color should be stronger, tinged with a dash of realism. For realism is an essential part of his greatness; and realism is quite simply a matter of the vitality, the energy, the tenacity, the willingness and competence to confront life without which he would not have become what he was and remains. We need only compare his habits of mind with Hölderlin's vulnerable spirit; his ambitious nature, destined as it was for the pinnacles of success, with Hölderlin's inability to throw himself into life and reality; his sturdiness with a temperament that could not endure the world, that was thrown off balance by every contact with vulgarity and could find refuge only in madness. In his poem *The Partition of the Earth* Schiller poignantly sang the poet's alienation on Jove's divided earth, and his destiny to be a native of loftier regions. Yet he regarded young Hölderlin as "a highly subjective idealist whose life turns deeper into himself and who is incapable of building the bridge to the contemporary world." And he wrote to Goethe, another member of the race of stout-minded poets: "Hölderlin possesses intense subjectivity, and with that a certain philosophical temper and melancholy. *His condition is dangerous*, for such natures are so ungovernable." This is the verdict of dispassionate sympathy. He himself, although a philosophical and artistic idealist, had no trace of enervating sentimentality, and was far more at home on earth than—with a touch of tender mockery—he allowed his late-coming poet to be.

For all his libertarian sentiments, there is a startling absence of sentimentality in Schiller's statements on politics and social problems. He did not limit himself to the celebrated pronouncement in which he flung the gauntlet into the face of democracy: "The majority is nonsense." He carried this further in his epigram, *Majestas populi*:

Majestät der Menschennatur! Dich soll ich beim Haufen
Suchen? Bei wenigen nur hast du von jeher gewohnt,
Einzelne wenige zählen, die übrigen alle sind blinde
Nieten; ihr leeres Gewühl hüllet die Treffer nur ein.

> Majesty of man's nature! Shall I see you in
> The crowd? Hitherto you have stayed with the
> minority.
> In this lottery few pay off; all the rest are blanks.
> And their empty commotion conceals the prizes
> from view.

Goethe was right in saying that Schiller had been far more
of an aristocrat than he himself; he departed from justice
when he added that Schiller had only watched his language
better. Schiller was not circumspect. Loving the gods of
Greece, he did not hesitate to give offense by voicing his distaste for the lonely Christian God who rules, friendless, without brothers or equals, upon Saturn's overturnèd throne.

Da die Götter menschlicher noch waren
Waren Menschen göttlicher.

> In the days when the gods were more human,
> Men were more divine.

He could be as blunt in his choice of language as he was in
his distich on *The Dignity of Man*:

Nichts mehr davon, ich bitt' euch. Zu essen gebt ihm, zu
wohnen;
Habt ihr die Blöße bedeckt, gibt sich die Würde von
selbst.

> No more of this, I pray you. Give him food and a
> roof o'er his head;
> Once you have covered his nakedness, dignity
> comes of itself.

But this is socialistic materialism, Heaven forbid! At any
rate, it is anything but the sweetness and light with which
popular fallacy charges him.

Schiller was never one to delude himself with shallow optimism. He was enough of a medical man to take the view
that idealism, the sacrifice of earthly happiness for the sake of
immortality, is rendered ironical by the corruption of the
body. In his poetry there are outbursts of bitterest despair
over the possibility of justice in the afterlife, of eternal reward for renunciation on earth. He states the choice between
hope and pleasure: "Let him who cannot believe enjoy; he
who can believe may renounce."

> *Du hast gehofft, dein Lohn ist abgetragen,*
> *Dein Glaube war dein zugewognes Glück.*
> *Du konntest deine Weisen fragen:*
> *Was man von der Minute ausgeschlagen,*
> *Gibt keine Ewigkeit zurück.*

>> Since you have hoped, you've taken home your
>> wages.
>> The faith you've had was your felicity.
>> Ask if you will opinions of the sages:
>> That from the book of hours no torn pages
>> Are given back in all eternity.

But this counsel of disillusionment is followed immediately by the *Ode to Joy*. And so the writer, with the flexibil-
ity of the creative spirit, passes at once from that melancholy
aspect of truth, from rue at the sacrifice of life to proud re-
affirmation of this selfsame sacrifice. For his felicity lay in
creative renunciation, and even at twenty-five he could declare: "When I think that perhaps in a hundred years and
more . . . my memory will be blessed and a tribute of tears
and admiration paid to me in my grave, I rejoice in my poet's
vocation and become reconciled to God and the frequent
hardships of my lot."

No, here is no languishing eternal adolescent, but a *man*,
tempered by the study of history, taught to be hard-headed
by the realities of the theater—which, at least according to his

own word, he mastered only late in life. He had finished
Mary Stuart, his sixth work for the stage, when he wrote: "I
am at last beginning to control the dramatic organism and to
understand my craft." The word "craft," incidentally, has a
notably hard-headed sound. The curious fact is that hitherto
he had not considered himself a confirmed playwright, and
for a long time was inclined to distinguish between poetic
drama and theater. In fact, he considered performable plays
only one department in the broad realm of the drama.
When he wrote *The Robbers* he declared that he "did
not aspire to be a playwright." He insisted on calling
this brilliant product of an authentically theatrical talent
not a drama but a "dramatic romance." He referred to
Don Carlos as a "dramatic poem," and maintained that
it was meant for reading and could never make a place
for itself on the stage, if only because of its length. For the
first edition had some hundreds more than six thousand verses,
and even after the final cutting there still remained more than
five thousand. It takes easily twice as long to play as an ordinary drama. Yet duration and dreariness are two different
matters, and the German theater apparently refuses to forgo
this closet drama with its splendid roles and its wonderfully
sustaining verse. Nor has the stage rejected *The Maid of Orleans*, though Duke Carl August remarked after reading it
that the thing was hardly playable. To which verdict Schiller agreed. *The Maid* became one of his greatest theatrical
triumphs, and the Leipzig performance, which he attended at
the age of forty-two, probably represented the peak of public acclaim. It was marked by trumpets and drums, torches
and cheers, as the audience formed a lane and hailed "Schiller,
the great man!" And he, who had long been severely ill,
passed through the crowds, tall of stature but stooped; powerful of frame but deficient in brawn; bearing on his face ennobled by suffering that expression of melancholy, friendli-
ness, earnestness, and absent-mindedness which Goethe has
described. As always, he was somewhat embarrassed by this

roaring success which he had not consciously "gone after," although seeking it was innate, part of his nature and his deepest will—as it was, some decades later, part of the nature and tyrannical will of that fellow theatrical genius Richard Wagner. For Schiller anticipated Wagner's comprehension and capture of the theater as a tremendously powerful, direct, tangible instrument of artistic expression. Schiller, like Wagner, invested this medium with deep thought, moralizing philosophy, the dignity of catharsis.

As he passed through the cheering crowds outside the theater in Leipzig he may have been reflecting how each such experience was essentially the same, how infallible was the enthusiasm inspired by all his actions, how mysteriously right his sense of drama, which rather took possession of him than he of it. He may have thought back to his first drama, *The Robbers*, and its extraordinary fate. By now, of course, the wild, boyish, in many respects absurd production struck him as unbearable. But it remained memorable to him, nevertheless, as the first milestone on his rapidly ascending career. He was only nineteen when he started work on it—a harassed and frustrated schoolboy suffering under the cruel discipline of a military academy administered by a prince who fancied himself a pedagogue, and thirsting for freedom and a more humane order. This youth's personal anguish and indignation brought to a focus all the outrages of the era, all the revolting aspects of a spurious society. He took advantage of his delicate health to report sick frequently, and lying in bed—a medical textbook held in readiness, in case someone should surprise him—he secretly wrote away at his drama. The greatest secrecy was essential, for "any tendency toward poesy is an offense against the rules of the Institution." And *what* poesy this was! His intention, which he confided to a few of his poetically inclined schoolmates, was: "We will make a book that the hangman will absolutely have to burn." And when he read it aloud to the boys, they listened open-mouthed with astonishment at his brashness. He read aloud to them in the

woods, and in the common room. Once, when he was presenting one of Franz Moor's scenes—running back and forth,
declaiming in excited tones and making desperate gesticula-
tions—Lieutenant Nies, one of the superior officers, poked
his head in the door and barked: "Why, boys, you should be
ashamed of yourselves for swearing that way!" There was
dead silence, and the lieutenant withdrew. "Old Nosy!"
Schiller called after him, while his friends chortled. Schiller
continued his play-acting in a more tempered voice.

Two years after he begins writing—by which time he has
been discharged from the academy and has become medical
officer of a Stuttgart regiment—the hangman's manuscript is
complete. But no one, naturally, will print it. The author has
to go into debt to the tune of one hundred and fifty florins—
and that debt is to oppress him for years—in order to print
the play at his own expense. But when the proofs come along,
he himself takes fright at his own audacities, and he begins
to tone down and delete. He sends the final proofs to Court
Bookseller Schwan in Mannheim, whom he knows slightly.
Schwan has previously refused to print the book, but now
that he reads it over, or perhaps really reads it for the first
time, something happens to him. The monstrous drama gives
him no rest, bowls him over, robs him of sleep. His mind is
afire with it; the word "genius" involuntarily leaps into his
thoughts. He takes the proofs to the director of the Court
theater, His Excellency von Dalberg, and reads the script
aloud to him. Schwan reads it to, or insists on its being read
by, everyone who counts at all: the director of the Regens-
burg theater, Imperial Councillor von Berberich; prominent
actors such as Iffland and Böck. The actors in particular show
signs of excitement. Naturally they think the ungainly creation has to be pruned into shape; but if they are given the op-
portunity to play in it, it might well make sensational theater.
Pressure is applied to Von Dalberg—who has, in any case,
come under the spell. This distinguished person writes a flat-
tering letter to the regimental surgeon in Stuttgart. If, he

declares, the author is willing to remove the most offensive excesses in his remarkable work, he is prepared to venture a production.

Schiller has never expected anything of the sort. His heart beats high. One of the foremost theaters in Germany is proposing to give substance to his ardent dreams and visions. In the meanwhile, eight hundred copies of the book—with the author's name rigorously withheld—have come onto the market. But he sits down to revise it for the theater, to sacrifice those Vulcanic elements which a pleasure-loving society cannot be expected to tolerate. The sacrifice is bitter, the work laborious; and, after all, the young man has other things to do. An epidemic of dysentery is raging in the military hospital. But he does what he can, does it as quickly as he can, and finishes—or rather thinks he has finished—only to learn that this trial is but the beginning of a process whose proportions he never imagined when he extended his little finger to the forces of established order. For they will take all five fingers, then will take the whole hand. His Excellency in Mannheim is by no means content with the concessions the author has already made. There must be more, more and more. In order to remove the play from the present, it will have to be dressed in historical costume, put back into the early sixteenth century, the age of Emperor Maximilian I and the Perpetual Public Peace in Germany. Schiller protests: "But my characters speak in far too modern and enlightened a way for that, especially my Franz, who is an intellectual villain, a cleverly metaphysical rascal. And Amalie is no knight's daughter! It will turn out to be a repulsive hodgepodge full of ridiculous incongruities, a crow with peacock's feathers!" But this does not trouble the worthies of the theater, and the poet has to bow to their exigencies. And since he himself has averred that he did not aspire to be a playwright, Herr von Dalberg takes the liberty of altering the text at his own discretion, toning it down, bowdlerizing it.

Then, at last, everything is ready for the performance.

And what happens? The theater is jammed for the *première*,
for rumors about the play have got around. Schiller is present, having slipped away from his regiment without leave.
And the audience, wild with enthusiasm, turns the theater
into a madhouse. Rolling eyes, clenched fists, hoarse out-
cries, strangers falling sobbing into each other's arms, women
tottering half fainting to the door—such was the scene in the
auditorium. The play had resisted everything that was done
to it. Its inner core had cried: "Go ahead, do what you like,
see if you can change me." It had been stripped, debilitated
ten times over, emasculated, despoiled, denatured. In spite of
everything, its immanent, innate vigor could not be killed; it
withstood all the timid precautions and has remained intact
to the present day.

That dynamic strength is not confined to *The Robbers*. I
saw *Love and Intrigue* in Munich after the First World War,
just after the Bavarian Soviet Republic had collapsed. The
audience was profoundly middle-class, reactionary and conservative; the performance was mediocre. And yet the fire of
the play threw this stodgy audience into a kind of revolutionary frenzy. The audience became Schiller fanatics, like
every audience that has ever witnessed his plays.

Of the three tremendous first fruits of his genius, *Love and
Intrigue* was the third. It had been preceded by *Fiesco*, that
tragedy of dissimulating ambition. While still a youth at the
academy Schiller had mentioned the hero of *Fiesco* by name
in his treatise on the relationship of man's spiritual to his animal nature. We are struck by the overlapping of ideas and
works, of the kind occasionally encountered in literary history; *Fiesco* followed so closely upon completion of *The
Robbers* that he must already have been thinking about it
while working on the first play. *Love and Intrigue*, although
not begun until after his flight from Stuttgart, was first conceived while he was still in that city. The idea can be traced
to those days he spent under arrest—the penalty imposed by

the Duke for his having again left his post without leave in
order to attend the second performance of *The Robbers* in
Mannheim. Profoundly embittered, he was in the most aus-
picious mood for developing a play in which he could lash at
the intrigues, the vices, the boudoir politics of a typical
eighteenth-century court.

In Bauerbach, living as guest of his motherly protectress,
Frau von Wolzogen, he worked diligently away at *Love and
Intrigue*, but during that period of arrest in Stuttgart he had
announced *Don Carlos, Infante of Spain* as his next dramatic project. At Bauerbach in 1783, at the age of twenty-
four, he finally decided to undertake this drama, and for its
sake laid aside the plans for a *Mary Stuart*, with which he had
already been toying for a considerable time—Mary Stuart's
turn was not to come again for another fifteen years, after the
completion of *Wallenstein*. In March 1783 he set to work on
Don Carlos, but broke off again the following month, since
Love and Intrigue was no further along than *Fiesco* had been
when he turned with sudden passion to the "bourgeois tragedy," as he called *Love and Intrigue*. He was not able to return to King Philip's court until the summer of the following
year. And how glad he must have been to forsake the bluster
of his Father Miller and begin with those noble lines:

> *Die schönen Tage in Aranjuez*
> *Sind nun zu Ende. Eure königliche Hoheit*
> *Verlassen es nicht heiterer.*

> The lovely days here in Aranjuez
> Are over now, and yet you, Royal Highness,
> Depart no merrier than when you came.

He looked back upon *Don Carlos* twenty years later when
he wrote in the preface to *The Bride of Messina*: "The em-
ployment of metrical language in itself brings us a long step
closer to poetic tragedy." But long before this, immediately
after those three powerful tragic efforts whose sonorous rhetoric was couched in prose, he had written: "A perfect drama

ought to be written in verse, as Wieland tells us; else it is
not perfect and cannot rival foreign productions for the
honor of our nation. . . . Believing as I do in the truth of
that dictum, I have cast this *Carlos* in iambics." What he was
sketching at the moment was as yet nothing more than a
genre painting of a royal family. But his political and dramatic instincts worked in unison; willy-nilly, he had to aug-
ment his picture, representing on the one hand stony scorn
for humanity and on the other nobler aspirations, ideals of
liberty and the good of nations. These resounded in his verse,
lending it not only oratorical splendor, but time and again an
incomparably moving tone.

> *Sagen Sie*
> *Ihm, daß er für die Träume seiner Jugend*
> *Soll Achtung tragen, wenn er Mann sein wird,*
> *Nicht öffnen soll dem tötenden Insekte*
> *Gerühmter besserer Vernunft das Herz*
> *Der zarten Götterblume– daß er nicht*
> *Soll irre werden, wenn des Staubes Weisheit*
> *Begeisterung, die Himmelstochter, lästert.*
> *Ich hab' es ihm zuvor gesagt.*

> Tell him
> That he should hold the visions of his youth
> In reverence, if he would be a man;
> That he must not expose the tender heart
> Of the celestial blossom to the killing
> Borer of reason, praised by all; that he
> Must not be led astray when groveling prudence
> Blasphemes that ardor which is heaven-born
> In us. I've told him so before.

Where is there anything finer, nobler, more stirring? The
man who wrote these lines is more than a rhetorician and
preacher. He is a poet who knows how to bring tears to our
eyes, while at the same time rousing us to indignation against
despotism. His express intention was "by representing the In-

quisition to avenge prostituted humanity and to fearfully pillory its ignominies." "I want to stab to the soul of a human breed which has hitherto only been grazed by the dagger of tragedy." And it is curious to think that all the while this great liberal carried secretly in his heart the figure of Mary Stuart, the lovely Catholic sinner, and all the sensual enchantment of her religion which he would have Mortimer invoke in song.

Don Carlos—how shall I ever forget the first passion for language kindled in me by its glorious verse when I was a boy of fifteen? The play transfixes one of the most engaging moments of Schiller's life as a poet, when he stood at the threshold of maturity and mastery. In the body of his work it occupies nearly the same position as *Lohengrin* in Wagner's, represents the same stage of development; and my affection for *Lohengrin* persists for much the same reasons. Echoes of the storm and stress of youth still ring in *Don Carlos*; later he will not indulge in such bloated metaphors as:

> *Durch labyrinthische Sophismen kriecht*
> *Mein unglücksel'ger Scharfsinn, bis er endlich*
> *Vor eines Abgrunds jähem Rande stutzt. . . .*

> My wretched cleverness creeps basely on
> Through labyrinthine sophisms until
> It halts upon the marge of an abyss. . . .

But what address, what fluency, what courtly polish, agility, scintillating *noblesse* and dramatic vigor of poetic line are found in this work by a young man of twenty-five! His verse is highly flexible, capable not only of accents of high emotion, but of a surprisingly natural speaking tone, as in the scene in which Philip sends for Posa:

> *Mich will er haben?—Mich?—Ich bin ihm nichts,*
> *Ich wahrlich nichts!—Mich hier in diesen Zimmern!*
> *Wie zwecklos und wie ungereimt. Was kann*

Ihm viel dran liegen, ob ich bin?—Sie sehen,
Es führt zu nichts.

He would see me?—Me?—I'm nothing to him,
Truly, nothing.—He wants me here in these rooms?
How pointless and how inexplicable.
How should he care that I exist? You see,
It leads to nothing.

This verse is capable also of compressing, with masterful economy, the poet's guiding credo in four lines:

Die Wahrheit *ist vorhanden für den Weisen,*
Die Schönheit *für ein fühlend Herz.* Sie beide
Gehören für einander. *Diesen Glauben*
Soll mir kein feiges Vorurteil zerstören.

Truth there is to benefit the wise,
And *beauty* for the feeling heart. Together
They belong to one another. May no craven
Prejudice crush this simple faith of mine.

He can also break up his verse with virtuoso skill into its rhythmic components and distribute the pieces among five or six voices, as he does in the scene outside the royal chamber, when Philip has lost the "human soul" for whose salvation he has implored Providence:

"*Graf, was ist geschehen?*
Sie sind ja blaß wie eine Leiche."
                                        "*Das*
Ist teufelisch!"
        "*Was denn? Was denn?*"
                        "*Was macht*
Der König?"
        "*Teufelisch? Was denn?*"
                        "*Der König hat*
Geweint."
        "*Geweint?*"
        "*Der König hat geweint?*"

"Count, what has happened?
Why, you are pale as any corpse."
                    "That
Is frightful!"
    "What is? What is?"
                    "What is
The king doing?"
    "Frightful? What is?"
                    "The king has
Wept."
    "Wept?"
    "The king has wept?"

And then Alba comes rushing out of the chamber, eyes flashing, and embraces the priest:

Lassen Sie
In allen Kirchen ein Te Deum tönen.
Der Sieg ist unser.

Now let
Them sing in all the churches a Te Deum.
The victory is ours.

Wagner, in order to put a greater distance between himself and grand opera, in which he had been schooled, would have no traffic with theatrical effects. But Schiller with his open-heartedness was able to restore innocence to such effects, to confer a noble naïveté upon them, so that we forget our supercilious smiles and rather bow our heads in reverence.

Schiller's language deserves a detailed study to itself, starting with those dramatic curtain lines of his: "It is possible to help the man"; "*Prince* Piccolomini"; "The Lord begs to be excused; he has embarked for France"—phrases all of the same order, and all peculiarly characteristic of Schiller. He invented a theatrical idiom of his own. Its intonations, gestures, and melodies are unmistakable, instantly recognizable as his; and it is the most brilliant, rhetorically stirring idiom that was ever created in Germany, perhaps in the world. It is a mixture of intellect and emotion, so full of the very spirit of the drama that it has become difficult since to speak from the stage without falling into Schilleresque language. His imitators did this in highly mediocre fashion. Emulation can spring only from true admiration. Ibsen was a great admirer of Schiller, and both his poeticized intellectualism and Wedekind's moralizing pathos of grotesquerie are far closer to the Schiller conception of drama than the slavishness of Wildenbruch and his ilk. At the same time we must remember the involved intellectuality of Schiller's language, especially in the works of his youth. It demands utmost concentration of the listener who wishes to follow it closely. Contemporary audiences thought *Fiesco* "too learned." That was only their ill-defined reaction to an intellectualism in diction hitherto unwonted in the theater. How those characters of his talk! They start right off in *The Robbers* where Franz, that deep-thinking rascal, is not the only intellectual. For they all speak in the grand manner, with ornate, cerebral emphasis; gentle Luise no less than Fiesco, Verrina and Karl Moor, and even that craggy German, the musician Miller. We cannot help wondering how much of this high-flown manner has passed into actual speech, or at least has rooted itself to the lips of the educated classes to remain there to this day, for all our current disavowal of literary and classical modes of thought. What has remained, at any rate, derives principally from the verse dramas; for verse favors the sententiousness to which Schiller is partial—too much so, some feel. Which brings us to his love for moralizing tirades, which have often been laughed at—but in his case wrongly, I feel. "The good man thinks last of himself" may sound hollow, but behind it there verily stands a man who really and always thought of himself and his own well-being last of all, and who devoted himself with high-hearted purity to a cause, to the ideals of humanity and culture. Or take that other well-known quotation—"Life is not the highest of all goods." That had previously been formulated in *Mary Stuart* in a more vigorous, more pungent epigram: "For base-souled men life is the only good."

We must speak also of the imperious virtuosity with which he dominates the iambic line, the noble, the incomparable music and splendor he confers upon it. He handles his verse with sovereign freedom; it does not matter to him if a line runs to six feet instead of five. He cuts it in half if he likes, or allows the meter to get completely out of hand, as in Thekla's lament for Max:

> *Da kommt das Schicksal—Roh und kalt*
> *Faßt es des Freundes zärtliche Gestalt*
> Und wirft ihn unter den Hufschlag *seiner Pferde.* . . .

> Then forth steps destiny, harsh and cold,
> Seizes his body in a fearful hold
> And throws it under the hoofs of his horses.

The very unevenness of the rhythm is onomatopoetic. Talbot's famous: *"Mit der Dummheit kämpfen Götter selbst vergebens"* ("With stupidity even gods contest in vain") begins unconcernedly with an anapaest. Schiller also introduces rough strokes of realism with equally virtuoso skill. These effectively contrast with the usual elevated tone, as when Wallenstein says: *"Und—wohl erwogen*, ich will es lieber doch nicht tun," ("And—thinking it over, I'd rather not do it after all.") Or: *"Prag! Sei's um Eger! Aber Prag!* Geht nicht." ("Prague! Take Egra, yes. But Prague? Won't do.") Or Max Piccolomini: *"Es* kann *nicht sein, kann* nicht *sein,* kann *nicht sein!* Siehst du, dass es nicht kann!" ("It *can* not be, can *not* be, *can* not be. *Don't you see it can't?"*) Or Octavio to Max: *"Max! Folg mir lieber gleich,* das ist doch besser." ("No, follow me at once, that will be better.") Or Wallenstein: *"Max, du kannst mich nicht verlassen! Es kann nicht sein, ich mag's und will's nicht glauben, dass mich der Max verlassen kann."* ("Max, you cannot leave me. I can't and will not believe that my Max can leave me.")

. . .

It is no accident that these examples have been drawn from *Wallenstein*, from that vast drama whose aesthetic problems troubled him exceedingly, over whose dense and almost unshapable mass of material he brooded so long. For that work differs in style and tone from all his others. Its cadences are splendid but unemphatic; it is realism confined within a framework of beauty; it is the product of that mixture of objective coolness and artistic enthusiasm which governed his relationship to the subject, and of which he speaks in his letters. "The material and theme," he says, "is so entirely outside myself that I can scarcely extract any liking for it. It leaves me almost cold and indifferent, and I am treating it—especially the principal character—merely with the artist's pure love. . . . Along the road I am following now it may easily happen that my *Wallenstein* will differ strangely from my previous plays by a certain dryness of manner. At any rate I need merely fear the extreme of sobriety, not, as formerly, the extreme of intoxication."

Only in this drama does Schiller's verse condescend to clumsiness, to using the language of the people and of servants:

> *"Den großen Kelch verlangt man, Kellermeister . . ."*
> *"Der auf des Friedrichs seine Königskrönung*
> *Vom Meister Wilhelm ist verfertigt worden?"*
> *"Ja, den! Den Umtrunk wollen sie mit halten."*

> "The great cup is the one that's wanted, Steward. . ."
> "Which at the coronation of King Frederick
> Was wrought so cleverly by Master William?"
> "Yes, that's the one. They want it for their toast."

But on the cup, the heavy gold cup, are "subtle matters delicately embossed." And the servants muster up a little history in explaining these symbols to one another. "There, on this first quarter, let me see." That Amazon on horseback is taking a leap over crozier and miter, and on a stick she carries a hat and a banner with the image of a chalice. What does this signify? It signifies the Free Election of the Bohemian crown. The hat is the pride of man, for

> *Wer*
> *Den Hut nicht sitzen lassen darf vor Kaisern*
> *Und Königen, der ist kein Mann der Freiheit.*

> A man who
> May not keep his hat on before kings
> And emperors is not a freeborn man.

And what about the chalice?

> *Der Kelch bezeugt die böhm'sche Kirchenfreiheit,*
> *Wie sie gewesen zu der Väter Zeit.*
> *Die Väter im Hussitenkrieg erstritten*
> *Sich dieses schöne Vorrecht übern Papst,*
> *Der keinem Laien gönnen will den Kelch.*
> *Nichts geht dem Utraquisten übern Kelch,*
> *Es ist ein köstlich Kleinod, hat dem Böhmen*
> *Sein teures Blut in mancher Schlacht gekostet.*

> The chalice stands for the Bohemian Church,
> Its freedom—for it was free in our forebears' times.
> Our fathers in the Hussite war compelled
> The Pope who would withhold the chalice from us
>   laymen
> To grant this noble privilege to them all.
> Utraquists prize the chalice above all else;
> It is their precious jewel; in many a battle
> Bohemians have spilled their blood for it.

The scroll above it shows the Charter-Majestat, the Bohemian Charter:

> *Den wir dem Kaiser Rudolf abgezwungen,*
> *Ein köstlich unschätzbares Pergament,*
> *Das frei Geläut' und offenen Gesang*
> *Dem neuen Glauben sichert wie dem alten.*

Which we once wrested from the Emperor Rudolf;
A precious, priceless parchment which assures
That the new faith, as freely as the old
May ring the bells and sing the psalms in peace.

That, to be sure, came to an end, and ever since Count-
Palatine Frederick lost crown and kingdom in the Battle of
Prague "our faith has lost its altar and its pulpit," and the
Emperor himself cut the Charter-Majestat to pieces with his
scissors.

Thus it was, thus it is; the people know their history well.
And on another quarter they see how the Emperor's councillors, Martiniz and Slawata, were hurled head over heels
from the castle at Prague, while Count Thurn, who had ordered the defenestration, stands by. That was a day. . . .

Schweigt mir von diesem Tag, es war der drei
Und zwanzigste des Mais, da man eintausend
Sechshundert schrieb und achtzehn. Ist mir's doch,
Als wär' es heut', und mit dem Unglückstag
Fing's an, das große Herzeleid des Landes.
Seit diesem Tag, es sind jetzt sechzehn Jahr,
Ist nimmer Fried' gewesen auf der Erden.

Oh, let me never more hear of that day.
It was the three and twentieth of May,
The year one thousand six hundred and eighteen.
It seems to me it were but yesterday.
And from that evil day it all began,
The heartache and the woe of our good land.
Full sixteen years have passed since that ill day
And there has never once been peace on earth.

So it stands in *The Piccolomini*, where he managed to tuck
it in, and this well-informed converse among the servants dis-
tantly reminds us of the exchange of basic facts among the
Norns, or between Mime and the Wanderer, in Wagner's
Ring. Good scenes these are, in themselves, but they also

serve the purpose of acquainting the audience with the complex background of the plot—mythical background in one case, historical in the other. As a matter of fact, in their genesis both these epics of the stage display a certain kinship. Both were originally intended to be single dramas: *Siegfrieds Tod* and *Die Wallensteiner*; and both ended by being divided into several evenings of theater. Wagner's musical tetralogy, like Schiller's dramatic trilogy, sprang from the sheer impossibility of compressing such a wealth of material into a single evening of theater of tolerable duration. In Schiller's case, many long and anxious consultations with Goethe preceded the decision to break up the play into a three-evening work—one of two evenings, rather, with a prelude. It was a fortunate thing for the poet that he was thus granted, at the behest of his great friend, freedom of movement through a full ten acts. An even happier outcome was this prelude, *Wallenstein's Camp*, first performed at the reopening of the Weimar theater in October 1798.

There were two especially troublesome points over which the poet had brooded while he tried to shape the unwieldy material of the drama. The first was the difficulty, in fact the impossibility, of bringing before the audience's eye or even imagination the army which was the very basis of Wallenstein's enterprise. The second was the poetic utility of the protagonist. For Wallenstein, this powerful figure who had exerted such fascination over his contemporaries, was also dim, ambiguous, mysteriously compounded of good and evil. Morbidly hesitant, led to destruction by the involutions of his own mind, he must, in Schiller's words, "never appear noble, never truly great, but always thoroughly terrible." Now, with a whole evening to devote to a tableau of the camp outside Pilsen, the first problem was solved. The poet was free to present in living form what otherwise would only have rumbled unseen in the wings: Wallenstein's blindly submissive creature and instrument which struck terror in the peasants, terror in the Emperor—that vast motley army brazenly consuming the fat of the land. And Schiller made the most of his subject, treating it with a deftness in form and a gusto which is astonishing in so tense a personality. Nothing else he ever wrote turned out as relaxed, as artistically sportive as these scenes. Incredibly enough, they were tossed off in *Knittelvers*, rhymed four-footed doggerel. They are full of blunt descriptions, of seemingly random strokes of historical color in which every word is evocative, every figure part of a tremendous whole. This whole was too extensive to be brought on any stage. The entire drama required compression of time and character, but this prelude in particular imposed on the poet the necessity of working in terse, symbolic terms. He selects therefore a few typical soldiers from regiments whose commanders will figure in the subsequent drama: a sergeant and bugler from Terzky's regiment, dragoons from Butler's, Croats from Isolani's, cuirassiers, arquebusiers, and uhlans from Pappenheim's, riflemen from Holki's. To these he adds a hard-bitten canteen woman who addresses everyone as "Sir" and will not charge for the drinks when a toast is drunk to Max Piccolomini, the young commander of the Pappenheimers; a camp schoolmaster and his boys; a Capuchin monk who lashes this wild crew with his lusty sermonizing in the style of Abraham a Santa Clara. They loiter around, gossiping, discussing, bickering, jostling one another, always on the verge of a brawl. And Schiller brilliantly suggests behind these few the whole vast army, carelessly living off the land, a rabble gathered from the four quarters of the continent, but nevertheless held in discipline and bound together in a proud sense of unity by the prestige of one man's powerful will. He makes us feel this, and more: the whole swashbuckling misery of that era of everlasting war, with its savage mercenaries, its smells of fire and lust, its riotous libertinage. Thus, with a degree of historical cynicism, he provides the picturesque, smoky background for the grand tragedy of nemesis which is to follow.

We must contest Tieck's assertion, in his highly ambiguous

critique of *Wallenstein*, that the prelude does not belong to the action of the drama; that it is mere depiction of "a" camp and its mood. Not at all! On a low plane, in the language of rough mercenary soldiers and from their point of view, all the elements of the coming action—or rather of the plot already in progress—are given. Every word reveals more of it: the dubious relationship of the army and its generalissimo to the Emperor, who has not entrusted him with this army but has rather received it from him on dangerous terms which make Wallenstein its supreme commander, indeed its absolute master.

> *Der führt's Kommando nicht wie ein Amt,*
> *Wie eine Gewalt, die vom Kaiser stammt!*

>> He acts like there's no limit on his command,
>> Like his power's not from the Emperor's hand.

The authorities in Vienna thought twelve thousand men enough for the General. But:

> *Die, sagt' er, die kann ich nicht ernähren;*
> *Aber ich will sechzigtausend werben,*
> *Die, weiß ich, werden nicht Hungers sterben.*

>> That many, said he, I could never feed,
>> But sixty thousand I will raise—
>> They won't go hungry many days.

This was the discovery of the age, the discovery of warfare that fed itself. And the mass army knew: "In the mass lies the spell of our might." If it were divided, reduced, weakened, its dread-inspiring force was lost, and the peasant would stand on his rights again.

> *Da schreiben sie uns in der Wiener Kanzlei*
> *Den Quartier- und den Küchenzettel,*
> *Und es ist wieder der alte Bettel.*

>> Then the Board in Vienna will write
>> Our billets for quarters and billets for mess.
>> We'll be beggars again, and make do with less.

In fact, before you know it they'll be taking away our general, for back at court they don't care so much for him, and if that happens things will look pretty grim.

Wer hilft uns dann wohl zu unserem Geld?
Sorgt, daß man uns die Kontrakte hält?

Then who will be there to see that we're paid?
Who'll force them to keep the promise they made?

For this reason the soldiers are wary of the bewigged old fellow from Vienna who has been seen nosing around everywhere since yesterday, with his golden chain from the Emperor. Rumor goes that he has brought His Lordship, who alone ought to be giving orders, such orders as this: that he must dispatch eight cavalry regiments to Flanders to reinforce the Spanish army which is preparing to march through Germany to the Netherlands. That is a cunning ruse! Spanish soldiers in Germany, soldiers over whom the general has no command!

Merkst du wohl? Sie trauen uns nicht,
Fürchten des Friedländers heimlich Gesicht . . .
Dem Kriegsstand kämen sie gern ans Leben;
Den Soldaten wollen sie niederhalten,
Daß sie alleine können walten . . .
Freilich! Es wird alles bankerott.
Viele von den Hauptleuten und Generalen
Stellten aus ihren eigenen Kassen
Die Regimenter, wollten sich sehen lassen,
Täten sich angreifen über Vermögen,
Dachten, es bring' ihnen großen Segen.
Und die alle sind um ihr Geld,
Wenn das Haupt, wenn der Herzog fällt.

Do you see what they're at? They don't trust our
    band.
They think Wallenstein has some secret plan. . . .
They'd like to end our preparations.

They want to hold the soldiers down
So they can rule the roost alone. . . .
But rest assured, we'll all be bankrupt yet.
Many a captain and colonel too
Raised a regiment from his own purse,
Put on a show, for better or worse,
Staked fortunes, strained every resource,
Thought it would turn out well, of course.
And they will lose their money, all,
If the General, the Duke, should fall.

Here the doggerel corresponds better than Tieck cares to
realize to the blank verse later on in the *Piccolomini*, when
Wallenstein's calculated resignation arouses general agitation.

Es tut mir leid um meine Obersten.
Noch seh' ich nicht, wie sie zu ihren vorgeschoss'nen
    Geldern,
Zum wohlverdienten Lohne kommen werden.

I am distressed for my commanders' sakes;
As yet I do not see how the money they advanced,
Or their well-deserved reward will be repaid.

And, similarly, the oath of unconditional loyalty to Wallenstein, which Illo and Terzky draw up in the *Piccolomini*,
is anticipated by the "*pro memoria*" drawn up in *Wallenstein's Camp* by the common soldiers:

Daß wir zusammen wollen bleiben,
Daß uns keine Gewalt noch List
Von dem Friedländer weg soll treiben,
Der ein Soldatenvater ist.

We'll stick together, come what may,
And neither force nor trickery
Can drive us from our Duke away,
Who's father to his soldiery.

The shadow of the man who has not yet put in an appearance lies mightily across this prelude. Around his head flash the lightnings of a Faustian demonism. The soldiers cannot help regard him with a simplehearted, superstitious gaze, for assuredly there must be "something behind" his power.

> *Der Feldherr ist wundersam geboren,*
> *Besonders hat er gar kitzlige Ohren,*
> *Kann die Katze nicht hören mauen,*
> *Und wenn der Hahn kräht, so macht's ihm Grauen.*

> Strange tales are told of his birth, it appears,
> And it's known he has specially sensitive ears.
> A cat's meowing gives him a shock
> And he starts aghast at a crowing cock.

But then, "he's one and the same with the lion in that."

> *Muß alles mausstill um ihn sein,*
> *Den Befehl haben alle Wachen;*
> *Denn er denkt gar tiefe Sachen.*

> Still as mice his men around him creep,
> The guards have orders to see to this,
> For he ponders on matters grave and deep.

All agree that fighting under his banner they have a "supernatural shield," and they are well content with this, for, no matter how dubious the nature of that shield, they feel protected under it.

> *Doch unter des Friedländers Kriegspanieren,*
> *Da bin ich gewiß, zu victorisieren.*
> *Er bannet das Glück, es muß ihm stehen. . . .*
> *Ja, er hat sich dem Teufel übergeben,*
> *Drum führen wir auch das lustige Leben.*

> But under the banner of Wallenstein,
> There I'm certain that victory's mine.
> He's taken Fortune in tow, you know. . . .
> He's sold himself to the minions of hell,
> But that's the reason we live so well.

They live well at his expense, so to speak, for Heaven will never demand an accounting of them, the common soldiers, for any pacts the Duke may have signed. Pacts there must be, for how otherwise could he be bulletproof, as was proved at the "bloody affair at Lützen" when he rode where the firing was thickest? But that is his business. Certainly it is not his elkskin tunic which stops the bullets; much more likely it is an ointment of witches' herbs, compounded and brewed with unholy spells. He is also bold enough to read the future in the stars—or, rather, it's not the stars he consults but a little gray man who comes to him in the dead of night, through bolted doors; after one of whose visits something big is always bound to take place.

There is no reason to assume that the man whom the soldiers discuss so familiarly, with a kind of horrified relish, would be perturbed at the aura of mystery and uncanniness which surrounds him in their eyes. A riddle to himself, he was quite the man deliberately to turn to use his mysterious relationship to himself, so that all others too would see him in the flickering light of incomprehensibility and say, as did his brother-in-law Count Terzky: "I often cannot make him out." This is what he wants; he likes it not at all when others wish to see his inner thoughts, or presume to imagine that they do. When Terzky says:

> *Was du bisher verhandelt mit dem Feind,*
> *Hätt' alles auch recht gut geschehn sein können,*
> *Wenn du nichts mehr damit gewollt, als ihn*
> *Zum besten haben. . . .*

> In all your dealings with the enemy
> You might have done with safety all you've done
> Had you meant nothing further than to gull
> him. . . .

Wallenstein freezes, retreats into his haughty, walled-off solitude, and replies:

Und woher weißt du, daß ich ihn nicht wirklich
Zum besten habe? Daß ich nicht euch alle
Zum besten habe? Kennst du mich so gut?
Ich wüßte nicht, daß ich mein Innerstes
Dir aufgetan. . . .

> And how can you be sure that I am not
> Gulling the enemy? Or that I'm not
> Gulling the lot of you? I do not know
> That I have ever willingly laid bare
> My inmost thoughts to you. . . .

Nothing could be more genuine. He is still the twenty-year-old of whom Gordon reminisces:

Durch unsre Mitte ging er stillen Geists,
Sich selber die Gesellschaft; nicht die Lust,
Die kindische, der Knaben, zog ihn an;
Doch oft ergriff's ihn plötzlich wundersam,
Und der geheimnisvollen Brust entfuhr,
Sinnvoll und leuchtend ein Gedankenstrahl,
Daß wir uns staunend ansahn, nicht recht wissend,
Ob Wahnsinn, ob ein Gott aus ihm gesprochen. . .

> He walked amidst us with a silent spirit,
> Communing with himself; nor did desire,
> The childish appetite of boys, attract him.
> And then there have been times when I have seen
>   him
> Transported on a sudden into utterance
> Of strange conceptions; kindling into splendor,
> His soul revealed itself, and he spoke so
> That we looked round perplexed at one another,
> Not knowing surely whether it were madness
> Or whether it were a god that spoke in him.

I am convinced of the accuracy of Schiller's portrait of Wallenstein, convinced that it shows the insight of genius, and cannot hold with those who maintain that the "real" Wallenstein was different. Schiller's historical and psycho-

logical intuitions have run boldly and unerringly ahead of
lagging research, which plods through the sources only to
confirm what the poet has already discovered. Kepler drew
up the real Wallenstein's horoscope, and perceived the decisive factors of his destiny in the conjunction of Saturn and
Jupiter in the first House of astrology, the House of Life. Instinctively, Schiller formed his picture of Wallenstein out of
this conjunction of Saturnian and Jovian elements, and the
result was a portrait of overpowering realism—one of the
most engrossing characters who ever stepped upon a stage.
Not that he is a hero who can arouse our enthusiasm or love,
whose ultimate downfall draws tears from our eyes. There is
no sentimentality in the poet's conception of his character;
only an amazing truthfulness which furnishes us with endless
food for thought, and an entire spectrum of meaning. Rarely
do we feel so strongly as we do in the presence of this character that the historian's task of showing, in Ranke's words,
"what actually happened" is in fact the special business of the
poet, at least in so far as innermost human motives are in
question.

Saturn: that stands for a darkly brooding nature, for inad-
missible thoughts fermenting in secrecy, for haughty disdain
of common human rules, for lack of interest in those very religious matters which were the passion of the age ("Why, no
one knows in what he really believes"), for emotional excess,
ruthlessness, unpredictable and frightening moods, somber
reveries, hunger for glory and power, caprice, and somnabu-
listic recklessness.

> *Nichts ist gemein in meines Schicksals Wegen,*
> *Noch in den Furchen meiner Hand. Wer möchte*
> *Mein Leben mir nach Menschenweise deuten?*

> The roads of my destiny show nought that's com-
>   mon,
> Nor do the lines upon my palm. Who dares
> Construe my life by any human signs?

This extra-human aspect of his nature strikes terror in others. But Jupiter adds to his sinister Saturnian half an element of royal command, the unmistakable trait of dominion, which engenders not only fear but also reverence, faith, and devotion. For in the end that element suggests goodness, rationality, benevolence toward men, in so far as it aims at *peace*—although that peace be one in which his power will prevail. He is a great general who, though born a Protestant, has performed remarkable military feats to maintain the Catholic Empire's hegemony in Europe. But he does not wage war for war's sake, and, if he can, avoids battle by diplomacy and by the mere threat of the gigantic army which has been attracted by the magic of his name. How right Max Piccolomini is when he says of him that

> *an Europas großem Besten*
> *Ihm mehr liegt als ein paar Hufen Landes*
> *Die Östreich mehr hat oder weniger.*

> He's more concerned
> For Europe's general good than a few hides
> Of land, more or less, for Austria.

Why should he be accused of treason because he "spares the Saxons and tries to awaken confidence in the enemy"—for is not that the only way to peace? Wallenstein is not dissembling when, in order to win over the Pappenheimers, he accuses Austria of not desiring peace and of seeking his ruin because he does seek peace.

> *Mir ist's allein ums Ganze. Seht! Ich hab*
> *Ein Herz, der Jammer dieses deutschen Volks*
> *Erbarmt mich. . .*
> *Seht! Fünfzehn Jahr schon brennt die Kriegesfackel,*
> *Und noch ist nirgends Stillstand. Schwed' und*
> *   Deutscher!*
> *Papist und Lutheraner! Keiner will*
> *Dem andern weichen! Jede Hand ist wider*

Die andre! Alles ist Partei und nirgends
Kein Richter! Sagt, wo soll das enden? wer
Dem Knäul entwirren, der, sich endlos selbst
Vermehrend, wächst—Er muß zerhauen werden.
Ich fühl's, daß ich der Mann des Schicksals bin,
Und hoff's mit eurer Hilfe zu vollführen.

My care is only for the whole: I have
A heart—it bleeds within me for the miseries
Of this German people. . . .
For fifteen years the torch of war has burned,
And still there is no pause. Swede and German,
Papist and Lutheran! Neither will give way
To the other; every hand's against the other,
Each one a litigant, and none a judge.
Where shall this end? Where's he that will unravel
This tangle, ever tangling more and more.
It must be cut asunder.
I feel that I am the man of destiny,
And trust, with your assistance, to accomplish it.

He is not dissembling when he deliberately employs the
"Jovian" element of his nature for Saturnian ends—that is to
say, to persuade the regiment to support the act of treason he
is contemplating. Both elements are equally genuine. The
historian Ranke tells us that early in Wallenstein's career,
when his troops were occupying a portion of Lower Saxony,
he combined military discipline with concern for the economic welfare of the territory. The result was a highly individual kind of occupation; he behaved less like a general than
like a prince paternally interested in his own principality.
This description of Ranke's accords completely with the
words of Schiller's Wallenstein:

Mich soll das Reich als seinen Schirmer ehren;
Reichsfürstlich mich erweisend, will ich würdig
Mich bei des Reiches Fürsten niedersetzen. . .

Let the Empire hail me as its shield!
And princely in my conduct, will I sit
As equal with the Princes of the Empire.

But if he who was once a simple nobleman and is now a
prince and duke should stretch his hand out for the royal
crown of Bohemia, it is doubtful that his inordinate ambition,
ever on the alert for the propitious hour, would rest content
with that. His soldiers in the camp have their own ideas on
that score. The sergeant says:

> *Ist nach dem Kaiser der nächste Mann,*
> *Und wer weiß, was er noch erreicht und ermißt,*
> *Denn noch nicht aller Tage Abend ist.*

> And after the Emperor, he is next.
> Who knows what more he may aim for or get?
> The full score hasn't been tallied yet.

If we remember that the lordship of Bohemia made one in
practice a candidate for election as emperor, we see that these
are not empty words.

The Jovian spirit, of which Wallenstein has innate understanding and which nevertheless is constantly opposed by the
Saturnian element in him, speaks forth magnificently in his
brooding monologue before he is to meet with the Swedish
colonel—that monologue in which he comes to terms with
the terrible import of his intention:

> *Und was ist dein Beginnen? Hast du dir's*
> *Auch redlich selbst bekannt? Du willst die Macht,*
> *Die ruhig, sicher thronende, erschüttern,*
> *Die in verjährt geheiligtem Besitz,*
> *In der Gewohnheit festgegründet ruht,*
> *Die an der Völker frommen Kinderglauben*
> *Mit tausend zähen Wurzeln sich befestigt.*

> What is your enterprise, your aim, your object?
> Have you honestly confessed it to yourself?
> You'd shake power seated safely on a throne,

Power on an ancient, consecrated throne,
Strong in possession, founded in all custom;
Power, by a thousand tough and stringy roots
Fixed to the people's pious nursery faith.

"Time consecrates," he reflects, and what is gray with age becomes sacred to men. And then "woe to him who lays irreverent hands upon venerable chattles, the dear inheritance of his forefathers." Never has a man haunted by ambition pondered so deeply his rashness in assailing the power and dignity of the existing order. And never has a traitor spoken with greater comprehension of the key role of loyalty and good faith in all human society, in all codes of conduct:

Die Treue, sag ich euch,
Ist jedem Menschen wie der nächste Blutsfreund;
Als ihren Rächer fühlt er sich geboren.

True faith, I tell you,
Must ever be the dearest friend of man;
His nature prompts him to avenge its betrayal.

He goes on to say that all the elements of evil which struggle and contend with one another suspend their conflict and league together against the common foe of humanity, the savage beast which cannot be brooked, which cannot coexist with life—faithlessness. And the man who speaks and thinks in such terms urges Butler, the upstart, to apply to Vienna for the title of count, and pretends to support the petition "with all the warmth of friendship," while in fact ridiculing Butler and recommending to the court that the man's conceit be trounced by an insulting rejection. And all this is a scheme designed to incite Butler to savage hostility toward the imperial house and fetter this man, so influential in the army, to his plans. And what about his relationship with Max Piccolomini? He loves this youth as a father and more than a father. He calls him the morning star of his best joys. When all desert him, he pleads heart-rendingly: "Max, remain with me.

Do not you, too, go from me, Max!" And when this noble
young man has found the death he sought as the sole way out
of the insoluble conflict of love and honor, there fall from
Wallenstein's lips those unforgettable words of grief which
far surpass in lyricism Thekla's too rationalistic: "Such is the
lot of beauty on this earth," his:

> Denn er stand neben mir wie meine Jugend,
> Er machte mir das Wirkliche zum Traum,
> Um die gemeine Deutlichkeit der Dinge
> Den goldnen Duft der Morgenröte webend.

> For oh, he stood beside me like my youth,
> Transformed for me the real to a dream,
> Clothing the palpable and the familiar
> With golden exhalations of the dawn.

And yet there is little doubt that Wallenstein has been dup-
ing Max, using him as a tool for his policies, quite as if the
boy were a Colonel Butler toward whom he felt no stirrings
of emotion. He sends him to escort his wife and daughter
back to Pilsen. He speculates on Thekla's lovely eyes and
Max's inflammable youth. He makes him vague promises of
his daughter's hand, although he is planning a far higher marriage for her. The girl suspects this. She says to her beloved:
"Don't trust them! They are false! Trust no one here but me.
I saw at once, they had a purpose. . . . Believe me, they are
only pretending to wish to make us happy, to realize our union." By "they" she means her father, whom she has met for
the first time this day, but whose true character she nevertheless knows. And when Max, in trustful adulation for his
Jovian commander, declares that "he wears no mask—he hates
all crooked words, he is so good, so noble," Thekla replies:
"*You* are that!"

The Saturnian element of Wallenstein's dual nature is in
the ascendancy in his dealings with his dearest friend, when
he tries to win that uncorrupted soul over to his policy of de-
fection from the Emperor. He plays an underhanded game,

and should not be surprised that he himself is the victim of
raison d'état on the part of Octavio Piccolomini, his conservative antagonist, in whom he feels a mystical confidence. His
bias for these Italians, the father and the son, which is re-
sented by many of his followers, was a trait of the historical
Wallenstein which Schiller faithfully reproduced. For the
historical Wallenstein was by culture and principle Italo-
European, supranational, and broadmindedly impartial in
matters of religion. His army was composed of soldiers of
different national origins and faiths. Whether a man was Papist or Protestant did not count; nothing mattered but capa-
bility in service and unconditional obedience to Wallenstein,
the commander. This was freethinking pragmatism in a
strange, contradictory union with his faith in astrological lore
and dreams. His relationship to Octavio, however, is founded
upon his mysticism. It constitutes a tragedy in itself. A second tragedy takes place between Octavio and his son; a third,
emotionally the deepest of all, between Wallenstein and Max.
No warnings will shake Wallenstein's confidence in the faithfulness of Octavio, his old comrade in arms. He is certain that
Octavio will follow him to the point of open treason against
the Emperor even while—and it seems almost incredible that
Wallenstein is not aware of it—Octavio remains with him
only to watch him, to see him ensnared in the net of treason,
to wait for final proof, and then to betray him.

Schiller resisted all temptation to picture Octavio Piccolomini as a scoundrel. This he is not. He is only a clever loyalist, a cool-headed worldy-wise diplomat in the service of a
legitimate order which he holds sacred. Pitted as he is against
a dangerously fascinating and intrepid adversary, he must to
defeat him have recourse not only to duplicity but also to
the courage of responsibility. The poet has endowed this
character with the same psychological verisimilitude and ultimately inscrutable ambivalence he has given his hero. But
we feel that Octavio's ambiguity, his particular compound of
aristocratic pride and craftiness, is on a lower aesthetic if not

moral plane than Wallenstein's. Piccolomini's betrayal of
Wallenstein's trust in him—a trust which he himself finds
hard to understand—is morally offensive.

> *Denken Sie nicht etwa*
> *Daß ich durch Lügenkünste, gleisnerische*
> *Gefälligheit in seine Gunst mich stahl,*
> *Durch Heuchelworte sein Vertrauen nähre.*
> *Befiehlt mir gleich die Klugheit und die Pflicht,*
> *Die ich dem Reich, dem Kaiser schuldig bin,*
> *Daß ich mein wahres Herz vor ihm verberge,*
> *Ein falsches hab ich niemals ihm geheuchelt!*

> But do not think
> That I by lying arts, by double-faced
> Complaisance stole my way into his favor,
> And nourished by hypocrisies his trust.
> Compelled by wisdom and that solemn duty
> Which we all owe the Empire and our sovereign
> To hide my truer feelings from this man,
> I've never duped him with base counterfeits.

Yet we must ask ourselves where the difference lies, where
the line runs between concealing true feelings and pretending to false ones. We sympathize fully with young Max when
he exclaims:

> *O diese Staatskunst, wie verwünsch' ich sie!*
> *Ihr werdet ihn durch eure Staatskunst noch*
> *Zu einem Schritte treiben—Ja, ihr könntet ihn,*
> *Weil ihr ihn schuldig wollt, noch schuldig machen.*

> Aye—this statecraft! Oh, how I curse it!
> You will some time, with your great statecraft,
> Compel him to misstep. It may well be
> Because you *want* his guilt you'll *make* him guilty.

And when the dreadful deed is done, when the Caesar has
been assassinated—an outcome which Octavio has not de-

sired, yet nevertheless has engineered—and Octavio is rewarded with the title of prince, his heart-stricken final gesture scarcely commends him to our sympathies any more
than does Elizabeth's after the execution of Mary Stuart. He
stands alone before the dropping curtain, a careerist in the
cause of law and order.

How much of tragedy this drama embraces, both on the
intimately human and the grandly historic scale! Tieck expressed regret that Schiller should have chosen Wallenstein's
character and fate for his theme, and thought he would have
done better had he made himself into a patriotic German
Shakespeare and explored the Thirty Years' War in a series
of dramas. In fact, however, he concentrated into *Wallenstein* the whole epoch of the religious wars, although often
he had to content himself with brief allusions, significant
catchwords, historical votive lights. The drama has a European purview, a universal scope, as do the thinking and the
operations of its hero; and it is all too easy to understand why
the mass of material over which the poet brooded seemed
"formless and endless" to him. "The more I define my ideas
on the form of the play," he wrote, "the more monstrous
seems to me the sheer mass which must be dominated. And
truly, *without a certain bold faith in myself* I should scarcely
be able to continue." This faith wavered often enough, for he
felt in himself the lack of "many of even those commonest
elements by which one brings life and men closer to oneself,
steps out of one's own narrow existence and upon a greater
stage." Who was he, he despaired, confined as he was and
without a world of his own, and where were his tools "to
comprehend an object so alien as the living scene, and especially the world of politics, is to me?" But these "tools" existed; they were his genius, which required only to be called
awake by poetic necessity, and his remarkable natural affinity
for politics and diplomacy. And so, in a trance of intuition,
he could compose a scene so fantastically acute as that between Wallenstein and the Swedish colonel. In its dramatic

alternation of mistrust and contingent agreement it is a masterpiece of diplomatic negotiation.

This dialogue in *Wallenstein's Death*, the great banquet act, and the earlier audience of Councillor Questenberg with its priceless exchange:

> *"Von welcher Zeit ist denn die Rede, Max?*
> *Ich hab' gar kein Gedächtnis mehr."*
> > *"Er meint*
> *Wie wir in Schlesien waren."*
> > *"So! so! so!*
> *Was aber hatten wir denn dort zu tun?"*
> *"Die Schweden draus zu schlagen und die Sachsen."*
> *"Recht! Über der Beschreibung da vergess' ich*
> *Den ganzen Krieg—Nur weiter fortgefahren!"*

> "Max, to what period of the war is he alluding?
> My recollection fails me here."
> > "He means
> When we were in Silesia."
> > "Aye! is it so!
> But what had we to do there?"
> > "To beat out
> The Swedes and Saxons from the province."
> > "True.
> In that description which the Councillor gave
> I seemed to have forgotten the whole war.
> Well, Sir, proceed."

—these three magnificent scenes may well be called the dramatic pillars of the entire drama. And it is a solace to every artist to see how a vast undertaking need not, thank God, be equally good at all points. That is not necessary, and utterly impossible. A few splendors like these three scenes, from which splendor radiates to the whole, suffice to hold it together, to redeem it.

We know how greatly the tremendous poetic drama gained, in general and in detail, from the presence of Goethe.

Schiller, communicative as he was, forever eager to elucidate everything, discussed it step by step with his friend. It
was Goethe, for example, who awakened him to the poetry
of astrology, which played such a part in the psyche of Wallenstein—for at the start Schiller was ill versed in this matter.
Had it not been for Goethe, who began the story of his own
life with an account of the constellation at his nativity, we
should scarcely possess that graceful exchange between Max
and Thekla on this occult world:

> *"Und jedes Große bringt uns Jupiter*
> *Noch diesen Tag, und Venus jedes Schöne. . ."*
> *"Es ist ein holder, freundlicher Gedanke,*
> *Daß über uns, in unermess'nen Höhn,*
> *Der Liebe Kranz aus funkelnden Gestirnen,*
> *Da wir erst wurden, schon geflochten ward."*

> " 'Tis Jupiter who brings whate'er is great,
> And Venus who brings everything that's fair!"
> "It is a gentle and an amiable thought
> That in immeasurable heights above us,
> At our first birth, the wreath of love was woven
> With sparkling stars for flowers."

But, whatever help his friend might offer, the enormous effort of realization, the struggle with poetic difficulties and
scruples, was the burden of Schiller's lonely nights. To master this monster of a subject cost him unspeakable toil, all the
more so because, as his letters complain, the work on it had
"no *suite*." It did not, that is, carry itself along; a day of flaming inspiration, in which he all at once saw in the passionate
light of genius what might ensue if only he had the good fortune to enjoy such grace always, had to be paid for by a week
of darkness and paralysis. Weary hours, these! How could he
distinguish between the effects of inclement weather, physical weakness and weariness from the harassments of an eternal cold, catarrhal fever, pains in his chest and abdomen—

between the effects of these and the faults of the work itself, which so often seemed to him a misguided undertaking, an ill-starred plan conceived in desperation? No wonder that he resorted to stimulants: liqueurs, fortified hot chocolate, a few glasses of champagne, and a great deal of coffee, in order to put himself into the proper mood for doing justice to the work, in order to hurl back for the moment the ennui which such persistent strain engenders. To overcome that ennui, desire, inspiration, and energy must be constantly renewed out of nervous reserves, out of loyalty to the subject and the ethical drive to finish what has been begun. Certainly these beverages were not good for him, and Goethe thought that certain passages in Schiller's work which were not quite just —pathological passages, he calls them—might be attributed to such intoxicants. In fact, Schiller scarcely practiced a healthful regimen. He was inveterately unwise about his sleep; he had become addicted to night work and would lie late abed in consequence. All his life he smoked heavily, and he would take snuff, although he knew better than his doctors—who tried to persuade him otherwise—that he suffered from consumption. He might well have been careless about husbanding his strength because he regarded his years as numbered anyhow and considered prudence in the conduct of his life as useless as it would be mean-spirited.

His was an accommodation to illness, an adjustment to living at peace with it. In his intellectual pride he would scarcely allow it to shadow his gaiety and audacity. Indeed, he occasionally expressed his gratitude to it, just as Nietzsche did. "Even chronic illness is good for something," he once wrote. "I have much to thank it for." Certainly he owed to it a refinement of the spirit, of sensibility and nerves. But still it is sad to read how a raw April destroyed "all pleasure in thinking and writing" for him, how ugly November days "stirred up all his ills, so that even work no longer gave him pleasure"—that work which was, after all, everything to him, for he was the most diligent of poets. "What counts most," he wrote in one letter, "is hard work; for that not only supplies the means of living; it alone gives value to life." It is almost incredible that immediately after completing *Wallenstein* he took up again his old plans for *Mary Stuart*. Without affording himself the slightest breathing-spell, he blocked out the outlines of this play, sketched the scenario, and finished the whole drama in the course of the same year that witnessed the first performances of the *Wallenstein* trilogy. And when this was done, he wrote: "I never feel so well as when my interest in a work is thoroughly alive. Therefore I have already made a start on a new one." The new one was *The Maid of Orleans*, the material for which was drawn from the *Curious Legal Cases* of Pitaval. *The Maid* was conceived as an operatic poem. As he wrote in a letter to Goethe: "I have always trusted that out of opera, as out of the choruses of the ancient festival of Bacchus, tragedy would liberate itself and develop in a nobler form. In opera, servile imitation of nature is dispensed with, and although this is allowed only as a special concession to operatic needs, here is nevertheless the avenue by which the ideal can steal its way back into the theater." Certainly the high-hearted, sublime play illustrates something of the sort. The ideal steals in under cover of the indulgence ordinarily granted only to opera. Schiller was always fond of rhyming his iambics at the conclusion of acts or scenes. In this play there is more music of rhyme than ever before; the blank verse forms only the fundament of a structure of poetic sonorities in which all rhythms vibrate, all the stops of language are pulled. There is a parade of the most variegated meters and strophic forms, a lively interplay between dramatic recitatives and lyrical arias. To inject, for once, the element of spectacle so dear to opera, Schiller also provides a grand and colorful festival procession to church. The element of the miraculous, of divine inspiration and prophetic vision, dominates the play. But then how is it that a scene like that in which Joan, a fettered prisoner, falls to her knees in desperate prayer, breaks her heavy chains, and speeds to turn the tide of a lost battle—how is it that this miracle seems no departure from the dictates of rationality, does not startle but only touches us, who find in it the beauty of a poetic conception? The answer is that we are here face to face with a different kind of miracle, a miracle of style. In spite of all the romanticism of the play, Schiller succeeds in preserving a basically classical attitude. If *The Maid* is romantic opera, it is that in a classical manner. It offers us the paradox of a classically restrained romanticism or a romanticized classicism—a unique phenomenon which delighted Goethe; for he applauded the tremendous success of the play and declared it to be Schiller's finest.

One would expect Goethe to be still more pleased by the far less theatrical *Bride of Messina*, on which the indefatigable Schiller now promptly "made a start." In the midst of his labors on *Wallenstein* he had dreamed of a strictly Greek tragedy in the manner of *Oedipus Rex*, but the next years had been taken up with *Mary Stuart* and *The Maid*. Not until the beginning of the new century—Schiller was then forty-two—do we hear again of the Greek play, that laboriously beautiful experiment. Its reintroduction of the Greek chorus sprang not only from a desire to imitate the ancients in all points more perfectly than Goethe had done in *Iphigenia*—for in the course of repeated readings Schiller had found Goethe's play so modern that he did not understand how it could ever have been compared with a Greek drama. His use of the chorus had a deeper purpose. He once wrote to Goethe: "Your own manner of alternating between commentary and drama is really enviable and admirable. In you both elements are completely separate, hence are expressed so purely as separate elements. . . . In me both modes are mixed, and scarcely to the advantage of the whole business." We must remember this when we read in the preface to *The Bride of Messina*: "The chorus purifies a tragic poem by separating reflection from the action, and by this very separation it arms itself with poetic force." This is the stringent analysis of the thinker *and* poet whose dualistic talent involved such aesthetic perils. In his great experiment he made a sharp division between contemplation and action, in order to equate the one poetically with the other by the very purity with which each was presented. And it is a fact that the intellectual brilliance of his verse rises to its pinnacle in the choruses of *The Bride of Messina.*

At the *première* of *William Tell* in Weimar a group of young people proposed a cheer to the author—a demonstration which would have been out of order in the Duke's residence. Schiller himself, quite out of countenance for fear of vexing the Court, shushed the enthusiasts, and the leader, a young scholar, received a reprimand from the police. The author of *The Robbers* had long since learned manners, in art and in life. Freedom remained the fundamental motif of his thought and his poetry. But the degree of his evolution since his beginnings is indicated by the very theme of the play. For what is represented but the struggle of a sensible people who waged their fight with manly moderation, steadiness, and respectability, when they might well have fallen prey to exaggerated and violent emotions? This was the play which he had been hoping for six years to write. There is a certain humor in the difference between the aims that animated him when he sketched out *The Robbers* and when he laid his plans for *William Tell.* This time "we" were no longer determined to write a book which the hangman would absolutely have to burn. Rather, he wrote: "And this must be a play which will net honor for us."—"It is going to be a tremendous thing and shake the stages of Germany."—"I promise you a real play for the *entire public*" (to Iffland). "My *Tell,* I think, is going to warm people's blood again. *They have an infernal hankering for such popular subjects.*" Here, then, is indubitably speculation on a grand scale, and an entrepreneur's practical eye to the theater and the taste of the public. Yet we can be sure that such naïve calculations were linked in his mind with the solemn determination to do good, with utter faithfulness to art.

In his famous, and incidentally highly offensive, review of Bürger's poems, Schiller exercised all his intelligence in pondering the problem of art and popularity. The people, he said, is a concept unstable in meaning. Our world is no longer that of Homer, in which all members of society stand upon approximately the same level of feeling and opinion. Nowadays there is a very great distance between the elite of a nation and the masses—one reason for this being that intellectual enlightenment and moral improvement constitute a coherent whole. "Aside from this cultural difference, there is also the matter of convention which makes the members of the nation so extremely dissimilar to one another in their modes of feeling and their expressions of feeling." Since, he continued, the people have long since ceased to represent a unity, a popular writer in our times must choose between the easiest or the hardest of tasks. Either he trims his work exclusively to the intellectual powers of the masses, and renounces the applause of the cultivated class—or else he attempts to bridge the tremendous gap between the two by the greatness of his art, thus to win both groups at once. Popularity, he argued, "far from making a writer's work easy or being a cloak for mediocrity," is simply one additional difficulty and "in truth so hard a task that its attainment can be called the highest triumph of genius. What an undertaking, to satisfy the refined taste of the connoisseur without making the work distasteful to the mass—to conform to the childlike minds of the people without sacrificing any of the dignity of art." He conceived of the popular soul as a torrent of emotion seeking speech. The poet who could express those affects, and at the same time provide for them a purer and superior glossary, who could intercept such feelings and ennoble them even as they fell crudely, formlessly, often bestially from the lips of the people—such a poet was for him "the enlightened, refined spokesman of the people's emotions." "If a poem with-

stands the test of genuine taste and combines with this merit
that of clarity and comprehensibility which makes it capable of living on the tongues of the people, the seal of perfection has been imprinted upon it." In other words: "What
pleases the elite is good; what pleases everybody is better
still." And, contrariwise, in poems intended for the people
the first question must always be: "Has any higher beauty
been sacrificed to popularity? Have they not lost interest for
the connoisseur to the degree that they have gained it for
the mass of the people?" This extraordinary critic demands
of such a poet a "gentle, ever equable, ever clear, virile
spirit," a spirit "initiated into the mysteries of beauty, nobility, and truth, which descends to the people in order to educate, but which never, even in the most intimate association
with them, is false to its heavenly derivation."

Precisely this is the spirit in which *William Tell* was written. The critic was able to meet his own requirements. He
set them up because he could meet them. His Swiss play is a
glorious work, plain, exuberant, and mighty, moving and
full of brilliant effects, first-rate theater and polished dramatic
poetry. Here, in truth, he succeeded in the hardest task of all:
in bridging cultural differences by his art. The play has won
the affection of the simple and the admiration of connois-
seurs—Schiller's formula for perfect popularity. This popularity has nothing to do with the "looking both ways" which
Nietzsche thought so disgusting in Wagner's art because it
represented a kind of cunning. Romanticism had always
aimed at union of popular with highbrow art; but its means
for accomplishing this were clever and debased: a mixture of
subtlety and childlike simplicity which imparts a quality of
corruptness to all romantic popular art. The whole charac-
terological difference between Schiller and Wagner, between nobility and ambitious cleverness, is inherent in this:
that in Schiller not a trace of cynicism can be found. What
he achieved in *Tell* was *classical popularity*.

Goethe, who had for a time considered writing an epic on

the Tell legend, called the story to Schiller's attention in the seventeen-nineties—once more, that is, while he was laboring on *Wallenstein*. Goethe afterward dropped the matter. But at the beginning of the new century rumors circulated that Schiller was working on a Tell drama, and this excited so much interest that prominent directors asked him about the play. The theme was still foreign to Schiller. It had not come from within himself, but had been handed to him; and a curious inner process must have taken place as he gradually accustomed himself to the thought that his friends were right in their expectations. Once again his habit of working on one thing and simultaneously sketching another appears. He was still busy with *The Bride of Messina* when he ordered fiom Cotta special maps of the Lake of the Four Cantons and its surroundings, and papered his room with them. Then he began studying sources—Johannes Müller's *Geschichte der Eidgenossenschaft* (*History of the Swiss Confederacy*), Tschudi's *Helvetian Chronicle* among others. How strange it is that even while his mind was dedicated to the tragedy with its Greek choruses, he was cultivating in himself affection for a subject in which he was initially not interested, which he had first to arrange and prepare for himself. More than once he called it an "accursed" subject, a "highly recalcitrant" one, which gave him great trouble, now attracting, now repelling him, until at last he became convinced that with it he would shake the theaters of Germany. A long time passed before he could turn seriously to this play which was to prove his most successful of all. He had only two years to live when he began it, and but one remained him when he finished. For, amazingly, he dashed it off in about nine months, from May to February, although he always had to "deduct from four to six weeks of miserable winter on account of illness or ill-humor." He dashed it off, and "succeeded excellently," in Goethe's opinion, though Goethe would certainly have done it quite differently, disliking, as he did, much of the play's seditious libertarianism, and later calling the scene with Duke

John, the murderer of the Emperor, an almost incomprehensible mistake. But he was astonished at Schiller's sheer in-
genuity in using the descriptions of landscape and atmosphere
which he had himself supplied. Schiller was not a man for
vivisection, for making studies on the spot. He did not want
to see anything and did not need to see anything. It did not
occur to him to visit Switzerland himself, though this would
have involved no great difficulties. Nevertheless, his poem is
a portrait of Switzerland to the life. Out of insight and intuition which required but the slightest external hints, he
brought forth the living people and the living land with its
rushing alpine streams, its lakes now sunnily smiling, now
suddenly lashed by the *Föhn* into mountainous waves, its
green meadows, villages, and farms, ringed round on high by
the eternal fortresses of cloud-wreathed mountain peaks, its
avalanches and glaciers, and the glow of perpetual snow. The
land lives in his drama by virtue of such incidental verses as:

> *Ein Ruffi ist gegangen*
> *Im Glarner Land, und eine ganze Seite*
> *Vom Glärnisch eingesunken.*

> In Glarus there has been a landslip, and
> A whole side of the Glärnisch has fallen in.

—lives in such terse and vivid descriptions of daily life as the
account that Armgard gives of her husband:

> *Ein armer*
> *Wildheuer, guter Herr, vom Rigiberge,*
> *Der über'm Abgrund weg das freie Gras*
> *Abmähet von den schroffen Felsenwänden,*
> *Wohin das Vieh sich nicht getraut zu steigen.*

> A poor hay-cutter of the Rigiberg
> Who on the very marge of the abyss
> Mows the ownerless grass from craggy shelves
> To which the very cattle dare not climb.

The persons of this play, enclosed in their superbly beautiful small world, these Walter Fürsts, Stauffachers, Melchtals, and the men who took the oath at Rütli, are certainly bathed in an idealistic light. But—and it is miraculous that the poet could hit it off without ever having seen them—they are undoubtedly, unmistakably Swiss. These rural folk are plainspoken, restrained, hard-headed, moderate, sober, by no means trained revolutionaries. They do not recite the Social Contract; they do not hold one hand upon their hearts and the other in the air. They want nothing but the rights they have inherited from their forefathers, which they feel to be sacredly linked to the natural world in which they live. These rights they will defend against intolerable tyranny. Though loyal to the Empire, they rise against the malpractices of the House of Austria. A more loyalist conspiracy than that of the Rütli men cannot be conceived. But although there is no hint of Jacobinism or revolutionary tribunals in their make-up, and although the time of the play is set at the beginning of the thirteenth century, it is nevertheless imbued with the atmosphere of the French Revolution. Schiller had turned his back upon the Revolution, but, in so far as it embodied the tie between national consciousness and liberty, it perforce remained, for all his horror of "the most terrible of terrors," the native climate of his emotions. *Tell* was banned during the Hitler era, but even in its own time there was much in it that "did not sound good to certain German ears." Schiller was once more compelled to make changes to tone it down. "I am sending you herewith, dearest friend," he wrote to Iffland, "the revised version of the three passages you found dubious. I hope that they now fulfill your requirements! I could not express myself differently without violating the spirit of the whole work, for when one has chosen a subject like William Tell, one must necessarily pluck certain strings which will not sound good to everyone's ears. If the passages as they now read cannot be spoken in a theater, Tell cannot be played at all in that theater, for then its whole tendency, innocent and just as it is, would inevitably give offense." For the Berlin performance he was asked to make further concessions and deletions. But the net effect differed in no wise from that of *The Robbers*; the spirit of the play could not be killed. And if we take the author's word that the play had a "greater effect than all the others," it owed the thunderous success which it had everywhere precisely to the libertarian sentiments that had seemed so dangerous.

How curious it is, though, that this poet always transposed his enthusiasm for liberty and liberation to other nations: to the Netherlands in *Don Carlos*, to France in *The Maid of Orleans*, to Switzerland in *William Tell*. This great German did not write a national drama of liberation for his own people; he deemed the Germans incapable of forming a nation and assigned to them, in place of nationalism, the task of educating themselves to be human beings pure and simple. This, of course, is no expression of contempt, for to represent humanity means more than to organize a national entity. The knottiness of the whole matter lies in his proclaiming that his people are destined for such representation; in telling them that they are chosen by the World Spirit to win out in the great movement of time, that their day in history will be the harvest of the ages, and their language will be the world's language because it can express the youthful spirit of Greece and the modern spirit of idealism. This *too* is nationalism, sublimated and raised to its highest power. All this and more of the same is to be found in an unfinished poem entitled *German Greatness*. It strongly reminds us of Dostoevsky's Pushkin address of 1880, in which the Russian ascribes to his nation the same destiny, often in the same words. In this speech Dostoevsky declares: "For what is the power of the Russian people's spirit, in its ultimate goals, if not the striving for universality and pan-humanism? . . . Yes, the destiny of Russian man is undoubtedly pan-European and universal. To the true Russian, Europe and the lot of the great Aryan race is as dear as Russia herself, as the fate of his native soil, for our

lot is universality; not that won by the sword, moreover, but
a universality achieved by virtue of fraternity and the striving for the unification of all men."

> *Das ist nicht des Deutschen Größe,*
> *Obzusiegen mit dem Schwert.*

> German greatness lies not in
> Winning victories with the sword.

Thus Schiller. He has always enjoyed great fame in Russia,
far greater than Goethe's. Dostoevsky in particular was an
enthusiastic admirer of Schiller. The lines from the *Ode to
Joy*:

> *Wollust ward dem Wurm gegeben*
> *Und der Cherub steht vor Gott*

> Rapture to the worm was given,
> And the cherub stands before God

so fascinated him that they are several times quoted in his
novels. When he reads his roll of great names, Schiller's is always among them. I have little doubt that the idea of the Russian nation's being destined to represent all of humanity—the
idea expressed in his Pushkin address, which opened the debate between the Slavophiles and the Westerners, is also a
"translation"—that it is German and derives from Schiller.

"If I can only reach my fiftieth year with unimpaired intellectual powers," Schiller wrote while working on *Tell*, "I
hope to be able to save enough so that my children will be
independent." Would nature grant him fulfillment of this
modest, fond-fatherly wish? In 1804, at the time he finished
Tell, it almost seemed so. He was "less hampered at work
than ever before, and very productive." In the summer, however—his wife was at this time expecting the birth of their
fourth child—he did not feel well. Painful cramps tormented
him until autumn. Then, however, he recovered and was
able to look forward with confidence to the coming winter.

It turned out to be a very strenuous time. A Russian princess, Maria Paulovna, came to Weimar. There were festivities; in great haste he had to write *Die Huldigung der Künste* (*The Homage of the Arts*), had to attend Court, the theater, balls. Violent catarrhs, a hazy state of mind resulting from colds, "smothered almost all his vitality." But then the following year, the year of his death, began with improvement and new hope. He was well in February, free of fever in March, regained his strength and was able to work on *Demetrius*, into which he had flung himself immediately after finishing *Tell*. It is touching to think that the marriage of the Crown Prince of Saxe-Weimar to the Russian princess played a part in the selection of this subject. *Demetrius* represents probably the most tremendous project he ever undertook. Its sweeping implications and enormous demands stirred his mind to an inspired delirium, while his physical state hovered on the edge of collapse. (When he died shortly afterward, the autopsy showed that the left lung had been completely destroyed, the chambers of the heart deformed, the liver hardened, the gall bladder unnaturally distended—in short, that all of his organs had ceased to function properly.) And still he went on working. He worked on the grandest scale, bore upon his already doomed shoulders the weight of craggy problems, undertook tasks such as even he had not yet confronted—the symbolic representation of masses and mass movements upon the stage. With incredible scrupulosity he drew up charts listing the factors against the play and for it. Among the former were that it involved politics; that the number and scatteredness of the characters detracted from interest; that it was of such a scale that it could scarcely be grasped; that it would be enormously difficult to perform. And finally, movingly, he added: "The vast amount of work." The positive factors were: the great point that faith in oneself generates faith in others, so that Demetrius becomes czar because he believes himself to be the czar. Furthermore, the subject appealed to him because of its sensuous variety and brilliance, its scenes of pomp and brutality, assassinations, battles, victories, ceremonies, and so forth. To its credit, too, was the exoticism of the material, the foreign landscape—all the more interesting because it was the soil of despotism—the complete novelty of a theme which had never before been treated on the stage. In short, in the end, the positive factors far outweighed the negative, even his trepidation over "the vast amount of work." He sketched out many pages in prose, wrote hundreds of verses, whole scenes—wrote because he was inspired and obsessed by the fearfully dramatic, morally shattering conception of a deceit which was no more nor less than shattered faith, of the necessity to live a lie. This theme of horror was more in Kleist's line than in Schiller's, but in the course of composition he so poured his heart into his theme that he achieved identification with his hero. Demetrius' searing monologue when he learns the truth about himself was completed in prose. He kills the bringer of the truth, saying: "You have pierced the heart of my life; you have wrested from me my faith in myself. Begone, courage and hope! Begone, joyous confidence in myself. Begone joy, trust, faith! I am caught in a lie. . . . I have broken with myself. *I am an enemy of humanity.* . . . Truth and I have parted forever! What? Shall I myself teach the people their error? The people believe in me; shall I plunge them into misfortune, into anarchy, defraud them of their faith? Shall I unmask myself as a deceiver?". . . "It is a secret he alone must bear."—"I must go forward, must stand firm, and yet I can no longer do so out of my own inner conviction. Killing and bloodshed must maintain me in my place. . . ."

His old character has disappeared; a tyrannical spirit has entered into him. His guilty conscience is manifested in his greater demands on others, his more despotic acts. Black suspicion fills his mind; he doubts everyone because he no longer believes in himself. Henceforth Demetrius is a tyrant, deceiver, scoundrel. And the poet puts himself into the minds of the others, who are astonished at this change. "How is this?" he has them think. "Has the imperial purple so quickly transformed his temper? Is it the new robes that have instilled this new spirit into him?" At this very point Demetrius has reached the pinnacle of fortune; everything has gone according to his wishes; there is no longer any resistance to him; all believe in him and acclaim him. His violent conduct is all the more striking because we would expect him to be lenient and serene.

It is plain that Schiller here has delineated the psychology of a state of ghastly mental stress. If we consider what faith in himself, in his genuineness and sincerity and in his humanitarian mission, means to an artist, a poet, then there is something fearful in the intensity with which such an artist at the height of his success, when everything has gone according to his wishes, when everyone believes in him and acclaims him, preoccupies himself with the theme of deceit, the theme of deception and delusion, with whose secret a soul parted for ever from the truth must live alone and go forward, in order not, by self-unmasking, to rend the people from its error, to tear down its enthusiastic faith and so plunge it into misfortune. And then that the author of all this, still struggling with this whole idea, so fraught with conflict and self-knowledge, shaping it with his last strength into a prodigious work of art —should die.

Nature, after much shilly-shallying, after reprieves almost incomprehensible in view of the physical condition of this man, who had been living solely on the resources of his mind, at last called an end to it all. But what a life this had been! Spent in never-desisting effort, always pushing forward, upward, in a state of *motus animi continuus*. That is how we must conceive it—the soul never flagging. He lived to be barely forty-six years old, and in twenty-seven of those years, inspired by continual studies, daily growing in cultivation, in knowledge of art, in his demands upon himself, he completed an opus that one who enjoyed Biblical longevity need not have been ashamed of. Here I have only been glancing at the crowning glories of that opus. For in addition to the twelve dramas, of which the last and probably the greatest remained a fragment, there are his poems. These are, to be sure, never lyrical; they are hymns sprung from meditation upon the destinies of man, upon historical and cultural subjects. There are also the ballads, which we must reread with fresh eyes if we are properly to appreciate their value; five or six of them are pieces known by heart by all cultivated Germans. In addition there are his prose works: the powerful *History of the Revolt of the Netherlands*, which followed *Don Carlos*, and the *History of the Thirty Years' War*, which preceded *Wallenstein*—Goethe was one day found weeping with admiration over this book. There are the essays and the critical reviews, all on the highest intellectual level. He wrote also novellas and short stories, among them the *Verbrecher aus verlorener Ehre*, the story of Johann Friedrich Schwan, who, his honor lost, became a robber chieftain—one further example of how attracted Schiller was by the abnormalities, bypaths, and quirks of the human psyche; in spirit, style, and technique this novella leads straight to the stories of Heinrich von Kleist. There is that wonderful novel, *The Ghost-seer*, which first appeared serially in *Thalia*, then as a fragment in book form. A suspense-racked public pleaded with the author to finish it; but he felt as little at home in the novel as in the lyric, and refused on the ground that to continue writing away at such a piece would be a "sinful waste of time." He was content with having shown how it could be done, how a storyteller with a gift for language could handle an intriguing, exciting entertainment on the larger scale. The story had to remain unfinished because it would gain nothing by being finished. He had enough to do for a hundred years. For in his desk, in his small, flimsy writing-chest, lay plans, drafts, preliminary notes on dramatic works of every imaginable theme, sketched out in more or less detail, in various stages of progress: *Die Malteser, Der Menschenfeind, Warbeck*—sixteen or seventeen in all, I believe. Had he had time for them, we would find him treading in entirely unexpected fields, espousing ever new methods of approach, perhaps presenting us with a completely different picture of his character as a poet. There were, for example, *Die Polizei*, or *Rosamund, die Braut der Hölle*, or *Das Schiff* and *Die Flibustier*—sea and travel adventures which he intended one day to tackle—he who had never seen the sea, any more than he had ever been in Switzerland. Besides all this there were two lists, mere notations of titles of dramas, subjects and alluring notions which he had at least momentarily considered for "the future." The quantity of these affords us some idea of the multitude of directions in which his endlessly tempted mind constantly strayed even while he was laboring devotedly upon the magnificent works which remain, completed, to form his opus.

But can I forget the earliest work of all, written while he was still at the military academy: *Semele*, the "operetta in two scenes" which, long before the surcharged prose of his three tremendous early plays, anticipated the blank verse of *Don Carlos*? This "operetta" of the passion of the creator for his creature was my first literary love. In its poetic structure and even in certain features of the language it points straight toward Kleist's *Amphitryon*. But such literary comparisons hardly occurred to me when I felt my first childish enthusiasm for the drama of:

> *"So lass' mich denn nie anders dich umarmen,*
> *Als wie—"*
> > *"Unglückliche, halt ein!"*
> *"Saturnia—"*
> > *"Verstumme!"*
> > > *"Dich umarmt!"*

> "Let me embrace you then in the same guise
> In which—"
> > "Unhappy one, oh stay!"

"Saturnia—"
"Be still!"
"Embraces you!"

(All of which, like the preceding scene of Juno's temptation of Semele, is but anticipation of Elsa's "Tell me your name!" and Lohengrin's "Stay!" and his "Woe, now all our bliss is fled!" in Wagner's opera.)

But take these words which young Schiller puts into the mouth of his Zeus:

> *Lang schmachtet' ich, mein weltbelastet Haupt*
> *An deinem Busen zu begraben, meine Sinnen*
> *Vom wilden Sturm der Weltregierung eingelullt,*
> *Und Zügel, Steu'r und Wagen weggeträumt,*
> *Und im Genuß der Seligkeit vergangen!*
>
> . . . .
>
> *Sie naht—Sie kommt—O Perle meiner Werke. . . .*

> I long have pined to rest
> My world-tormented head upon thy breast—
> To lull my wearied senses to repose
> From the wild storm of godly rule and woes,
> To dream away the emblems of my might,
> My reins, my tiller, and my chariot bright,
> And live for nought beyond the joys of love!
>
> . . . .
>
> She comes—draws near—the pearl of all my works. . . .

Has no professor of literature yet recognized in these verses the "world-ordering" agonizedly yearning head of Kleist's Jupiter with his "my adored creature," "my idol," and his melancholic creator's plea:

> *So viele Freude schüttet*
> *Er zwischen Erd' und Himmel endlos aus;*
> *Wärst du vom Schicksal nun bestimmt,*

So vieler Millionen Wesen Dank,
Ihm seine ganze Ford'rung an die Schöpfung
In einem einz'gen Lächeln auszuzahlen,
Würd'st du dich ihm wohl—ach!

So much joy unending
He lavishes between the earth and heaven;
If now you were by destiny appointed
To give thanks for so many million beings,
To pay all that creation owes to him
Now all at once, within a single smile,
Think you you would—ah!

But enough of *Semele*. Enough of first things and last things. Only once more we must exclaim: What a life this was! The figures of women pass through it, some for a fleeting moment, some making deeper inroads upon the senses and the heart. In Bauerbach there was his patroness Henriette von Wolzogen's sixteen-year-old daughter Lotte, who awoke dreams of happiness in the twenty-three-year-old poet, for some of his deeply felt respect and gratitude toward the mother was transferred to the charming young girl. Lotte made some passive contribution to the lifelikeness of his Luise Miller in *Love and Intrigue*; in his tenderness for her, this boy who had grown up in the male atmosphere of a barracks won a little insight into femininity. The experience also gave him a personal acquaintance with that cruel barrier of class separating two lovers which forms the theme of the play. Lotte von Wolzogen was quite sensible. She went along with society's dictates, and elected to love and marry a young army officer of the nobility instead of the middle-class poet. Whereupon the feelings her admirer had had for her died a fairly quick and painless death. But in Mannheim two years later another Charlotte came into his life. She bore the name he had given to the foolish lord chamberlain in *Love and Intrigue*, Von Kalb, and was also of noble birth, likewise related to Frau von Wolzogen. She happened, moreover, to be married to a major in the French army; but her marriage could not have been a particularly happy one, as her receptivity to the poet's homage seems to prove. This was a serious and longer-lasting emotional involvement, for Frau von Kalb was a woman of superior stature, acquainted with suffering and solitude, craving the intellectual life, influenced both by Catholic mysticism and Pietism. Their relations went quite far, but at the last moment, out of religious scruples or Heaven only knows what else, she would not give herself to him. Thus it ended; but once again art profited by the poet's experience: in *Don Carlos* certain features of both the Queen and Princess Eboli are borrowed from this Charlotte.

Schiller was twenty-eight when he saw a young beauty at a masked ball in Dresden. Once again she was a noblewoman —Henriette von Arnim. She was a dazzling creature, intoxicating to the senses, but so deficient otherwise, so emptyheaded and bent on nothing but pleasure, that his passion for her subsided as rapidly as it had kindled.

Inevitably, actresses who played parts in his dramas "interested" him at times; his biographers mention three or four names. One, Sophie Albrecht, he wished to "save from the theater"—in practice, then, the theater did not exactly seem to him a "moral institution." Rumor had it that he even intended to marry a certain Katharina Baumann, but rumor proved false. It was nearer right about Margarete Schwan, daughter of a publisher, a strikingly pretty, elegant, and cultivated girl of eighteen. The attachment went painfully deep this time—painfully because the demoiselle proved to be a second Henriette, coldhearted, flirtatious, spoiled by attentions. And so, not for the first time, Schiller experienced the suffering and shame of an unworthy passion. For a while he entertained the thought of asking for the hand of Wieland's daughter, Wilhelmine. But this would merely have been for social reasons; he did not love the girl.

In Rudolstadt, Wilhelm von Wolzogen had introduced him to the Lengefeld family, whom he had met briefly once

before in Mannheim. Now the two daughters of the house,
Caroline and Charlotte, made a deep impression upon him—
Caroline as well, although she was married, Wolzogen himself having become her second husband. Probably she interested Schiller more than her sister, for she was a complex
woman, unhappy in both marriages and as a personality superior to her maidenly sister. But the latter was charming and
simple, of a harmonious spirit; in time she drew the confidence and affection of the poet. Moreover, she was free. And
so the choice fell upon her; she became his wife and the
mother of his children. At twenty-eight he had written: "If I
reach thirty unmarried, I shall not marry. Already I have lost
my inclination to do so. A woman of superior merits does not
make me happy, or I do not know myself." Now, three years
later, he has changed his tune: "How different to live at the
side of a dear wife from being forsaken and alone. . . .
What a lovely life I lead now. I look about me with gaiety,
and my heart finds continual peaceful satisfaction outside itself, my mind is nourished and refreshed by loveliness. My
life has entered a phase of harmonious equanimity; the passionate tension is gone, and my days pass by peacefully and
clearly. I look toward the future with serene courage. . . ."
How good it is to read this. How good to see this forever
restless, thought-haunted, sublime stepchild of life who said
of himself: "Whatever I am I have become through an often
unnatural tensing of my powers"—how good to see him for
once relaxed, for once in a state of quiet and serene contentment. To see him for once enjoying the ordinary happiness
of humanity, the repose he so long had yearned for.

He had, then, undergone a few rather tame temptations,
had felt some stirrings of the deeper emotions, and then made
his peace, found the haven of marriage. In that unlyric life of
his, eroticism played no creative part. Unlike Goethe's, his
biography cannot be divided into periods under the aegis of
a particular woman. There is no Sesenheim or Wetzlar, no
Lida, Marianne, or Ulrike. In him the polarity of the sexes

was transformed into intellectual terms, as was everything else. The great adventure of his life, his experience with passionate attraction and repulsion, with deep hostility, deep yearning and admiration, with giving and taking, with jealousy, downcast envy and proud self-assertiveness, with long-lasting emotional tension—was an affair between man and man, between himself, who was so essentially masculine, and that other poet to whom he was inclined to attribute a feminine disposition (though others, such as Schlegel, stressed precisely the latter's masculinity). The great adventure of his life was his relationship with Goethe.

This relationship is the central chapter of his biography. The friendship founded on the polarity of opposite tempers had tremendous importance for Goethe also, as he frequently testified, particularly after Schiller's death. But the one who truly fell prey to it, who struggled with it, was always deeply preoccupied with it, for whom it took the place of the sufferings and joys of erotic love, was Schiller. Goethe's part in it was cool and unemotional compared to the persistent hate-love of Schiller, who reproached the other for his egotism, spoke of him as if he were some coy and self-willed beauty who must be "knocked up" if she is to be held. Schiller was wholly the suitor; his fevered antithetical thought processes were entirely determined by the existence of the other. His feelings for Goethe were poured out in intellectualized poetry replete with a troubled humility, though also with uncompromising manly dignity. Thus, in his poems he gave second place to the heroic toil which was his own lot, first to the gifts which came so naturally to Goethe. He was at pains not to resent the difference.

It is strange that when people speak of Schiller's poetry they scarcely ever mention that inexpressibly moving poem in distichs in which for once he is truly a lyricist. Controlled though it is, it is his most deeply felt poem and, in its noble resignation, his most beautiful. I speak of *Fortune*, that eu-

logy of the man whom the gracious gods loved even before
his birth, and whom as an infant Venus rocked in her arms.

Welchem Phöbus die Augen, die Lippen Hermes gelöset
Und das Siegel der Macht Zeus auf die Stirne gedrückt!
Ein erhabenes Los, ein göttliches, ist ihm gefallen,
Schon vor des Kampfes Beginn sind ihm die Schläfen
bekränzt.
Ihm ist, eh' er es lebte, das volle Leben gerechnet,
Eh' er die Mühe bestand, hat er die Charis erlangt.

Phoebus has shaped his eyes, his lips are chiseled by
Hermes,
And the signet of might Zeus has impressed on his
brow!
What an illustrious fate, what a godlike future
awaits him;
Ere the strife has begun gaily his temples are
crowned.
Ere he has lived, to him the measure of life is
awarded,
Ere he has toiled in the vineyard, the Graces have
flown to his aid.

And then Schiller speaks of himself.

Groß zwar nenn' ich den Mann, der, sein eigner Bildner
und Schöpfer,
Durch der Tugend Gewalt selber die Parze bezwingt;
Aber nicht erzwingt er das Glück, und was ihm die
Charis
Neidisch geweigert, erringt nimmer der strebende Mut.
Vor Unwürdigem kann dich der Wille, der ernste, be-
wahren,
Alles Höchste, es kommt frei von den Göttern
herab. . . .
Zürne dem Glücklichen nicht, daß den leichten Sieg
ihm die Götter

Schenken, daß aus der Schlacht Venus den Liebling ent-
rückt. . . .
Zürne der Schönheit nicht, daß sie schön ist, daß sie
verdienstlos
Wie der Lilie Kelch, prangt durch der Venus Geschenk!
Lass' sie die Glückliche sein, du schaust sie, du bist der
Beglückte!
Wie sie ohne Verdienst glänzt, so entzücket sie
dich. . . .

> *Surely the man is great* who has shaped and created
> himself
> And by Virtue's aid, singly encounters the Fates.
> Fortune alone he fails to compel; what the Graces
> deny him
> Enviously, neither ambition nor valor will win for
> him.
> From whatever is base, an earnest will can preserve
> you;
> All that is highest the gods freely and amply be-
> stow. . . .
> Grudge not the fortunate man that the gods have
> aided his triumph
> Or that Venus has snatched her favorite from the
> fray. . . .
> Grudge not the beauty her beauty, and that with-
> out effort she
> Thanks to Venus's gifts shines fair as the cup of the
> lily.
> Let her be the fortunate one; her fortune is yours
> when you see her.
> That she is so easily fair adds to the pleasure she
> gives you. . . .

Shall I continue to quote? The temptation is great. Let me
add only this:

*Auf dem geschäftigen Markt, da führe Themis die
Waage,
Und es messe der Lohn streng an der Mühe sich ab. . . .
Alles Menschliche muß erst werden und wachsen und
reifen,
Und von Gestalt zu Gestalt führt es die bildende Zeit;
Aber das Glückliche siehest du nicht, das Schöne nicht
werden.
Fertig von Ewigkeit her steht es vollendet vor dir.
Jede irdische Venus ersteht, wie die erste des Himmels,
Eine dunkle Geburt, aus dem unendlichen Meer;
Wie die erste Minerva, so tritt, mit der Ägis gerüstet,
Aus des Donnerers Haupt jeder Gedanke des Lichts.*

> Guarding the busy exchange, let Themis attend
> with her balance
> And mete out the reward strictly according to
> toil. . . .
> All that is human must first be born, grow fuller
> and ripen,
> Time with his shaping hand leads all from stage to
> stage;
> But neither Fortune nor beauty can you mark as
> they come into being;
> All complete they are, born of Eternity's womb.
> Every Venus of earth, like the Venus of heaven,
> arises,
> A mysterious birth, out of the depths of the sea.
> Just as Minerva of old came forth equipped with
> her aegis
> Springs from the Thunderer's brow every luminous
> thought.

Nothing more beautiful, more elevated, more sanctified
can be found in the whole realm of emotion and of language.
I would give whole anthologies of erotic poetry for this love-
song of mind, of will, this song written by the toiler in the

vineyard, the man of effort and virtue, to the effortless partaker of divinity; the song of the contemplative spirit to the spirit which in itself is all that may be contemplated. To be sure, Goethe's *Epilogue to The Bell* rounds out the psychological portrait, returns admiration for admiration; but this poem, *Das Glück*, remains the supreme poetic monument to a magnificent and complex friendship. The poem is the sublimation and ultimate spiritualization of all the bitterness and smarting rancor which the generous man of virtue must feel when confronted with the mysterious nonchalance of daemonic natural gifts. Schiller tasted that bitterness to the dregs. "To be about Goethe often would make me unhappy," he confides in a letter in 1789. "Even toward his closest friends he never for a moment unburdens himself. There is nowhere that one can grasp him. I believe, in fact, that he is an egotist to an extraordinary degree. . . . That aspect of him is odious to me, although at the same time I love his mind with all my heart and have the highest opinion of him. He has aroused in me a curious mixture of hatred and love, a feeling not unlike that which Brutus and Cassius must have had toward Caesar. I could assassinate his mind and once again love it with all my heart. His judgment matters enormously to me. . . . I would like to surround him with eavesdroppers, for I know I shall never bring myself to ask him what he thinks of me." That flash of dramatic intrigue —"surround him with eavesdroppers"—is genuine Schiller, and so is the ambivalent affection. For example, he writes in the same year: "Goethe is simply in my way, and reminds me so frequently that fate has used me unkindly. How destiny has fostered his genius, while I have had to fight and go on fighting to this very minute." Or a year later: "It is interesting to see how Goethe clothes everything in his own particular mode and gives out again, in strangely altered fashion, what he has read; but I nevertheless prefer not to dispute with him about things which interest me deeply. *He lacks entirely the straightforwardness to take a stand on anything.*

To him all of philosophy is subjective, and that view puts an end to belief and debate."

This sorrow over Goethe's evasion of commitment was never entirely dispelled, even during those periods in which he spoke to Goethe himself of the "fine relationship between us" and, almost echoing Goethe's aphorism, declared: "Toward the man of excellence the only freedom is love." It was there still when he wrote to others about his friend: "The lofty merits of his mind are not what bind me to him. If he did not have, as a person, the greatest worth of anyone I have ever met, I would admire his genius only from afar. I may say that in the six years I have associated with him I have never for a moment doubted his character. There is a high truthfulness and rectitude in his nature, and the deepest concern for justice and goodness; that is why gossips and hypocrites and sophists have always felt ill at ease in his presence. . . ." Schiller, with his pure heart, had no need to feel qualms in the presence of rectitude and concern for justice and goodness, though he was prone to worry over his friend's sublime indifference, which resembled that of blind nature herself. And what satisfaction it was that intellect could *help* nature, that the hero could assist the god, encourage and spur him on, elucidate and vanquish his obscure hesitations, display toward him a bit of friendly superiority. There were moments, as in their discussions of the problems of *Faust*, at which intellect, philosophy, the idea, triumphed over divine naïveté—or appeared so to triumph. With a kind of sublime malice Schiller would see his beloved antagonist forced to wrestle with the questions he himself had so laboriously mastered. "The requirements of *Faust* are simultaneously poetical and philosophical; twist and turn as you will, the nature of the subject will impose upon you a philosophical treatment, and imagination will have to accommodate to the service of a rational idea." Well, when all was said and done, no such accommodation took place; within the flexible framework of his cosmic poem Goethe somehow escaped the bid-

dings of a rational idea. "Idea?" he asked in his old age. "Not
that I know of. They come and ask what idea I have tried to
embody in my *Faust*. As if I myself knew or could say! From
Heaven through the world to Hell—that might be said of it
at a pinch; but that is no idea; rather that happens to be the
story. . . . It really would have been a fine mess if I had attempted to string so rich, colorful, and variegated a thing as
my *Faust* upon the slender cord of a single continuous idea."

Still and all, he could write to Schiller: "You have given
me a second youth, made me a poet again." This may have
salved the feelings of the younger poet whose impulsive salu-
tation "Beloved Friend," used in one letter only, was never
reciprocated by Goethe. And was it not also true of Schiller
that after having been lost for so long in abstractions he was
once more "made a poet again"? For him it was a most fruitful kind of stimulus to observe Goethe's specific genius, to see
art as a force of nature, to be following the inner workings of
an intuitive man. Theirs was a truly great exchange; their admiration was mutual, and on Goethe's part it grew steadily
after Schiller's death. It is as though he never fully realized, as
long as Schiller was alive, what he meant to him. There is no
doubt that he had loved him during his lifetime also, though
at times he shook his head in charitable deprecation. He stood
guard over Schiller's sensitive feelings. Thus, in company he
would steer the conversation in a new direction when he noticed that his friend was unhappy with the turn it was taking.
He would make opportunities for his friend to take the floor
and shine. Nothing in his poetry of that period corresponds
in depth of feeling to Schiller's poem on *Fortune*. But late in
life, in the Chiron scene in the Second Part of *Faust*, where
there is talk of "the august company of Argonauts," he suddenly gave expression to a comparable emotion. It is veiled,
certainly, but its import can scarcely be mistaken.

> *So wirst du mir denn doch gestehn:*
> *Du hast die Größten deiner Zeit gesehn . . .*

Doch unter den heroischen Gestalten,
Wen hast du für den Tüchtigsten gehalten?

You must admit, say what you may,
You saw the greatest heroes of your day. . . .
But among all those forms heroical
Whom did you hold the worthiest of all?

The centaur names all of them, saying that "each was worthy
after his own fashion," and Faust asks: "And Hercules? Why
not mention him?" Chiron replies:

O Weh! Errege nicht mein Sehnen!
Ich hatte Phöbus nie gesehn,
Noch Ares, Hermes, wie sie heißen;
Da sah ich mir vor Augen stehn,
Was alle Menschen göttlich preisen.
So war er ein geborner König. . . .

Oh! Do not cause my eyes to swim.
Phoebus I had never seen
Nor Ares, Hermes, and their kind;
But then I saw—and saw it plain—
What all men praise and god-like find.
He was so born to be a king. . . .

Who was this Hercules, whom poets strive in vain to cele-
brate, for whom sculptors "vainly torture stone"? We think
we know—indeed, we do know.

Goethe, then, beheld his late friend as a Hercules, the hero
of the twelve labors who was raised up among the gods. This
suggests that he knew of Schiller's long-cherished project of
an Olympian idyll treating of the heavenly wedding of Hercules with Hebe, the goddess who pours out the ambrosia of
eternal youth. This concept lingered in the poet's mind as
the supreme, the ultimate subject. As far as I know, it is not
set down in any of his notes or outlines; but its theme is
sounded in the final stanza of *Das Ideal und das Leben* (*Ideal
and Life*):

Bis der Gott, des Irdischen entkleidet,
Flammend sich vom Menschen scheidet
Und des Äthers leichte Lüfte trinkt.
Froh des neuen ungewohnten Schwebens
Fließt er aufwärts, und des Erdenlebens
Schweres Traumbild sinkt und sinkt und sinkt.
Des Olympus Harmonien empfangen
Den Verklärten in Kronions Saal,
Und die Göttin mit den Rosenwangen
Reicht ihm lächelnd den Pokal.

Until the god throws off his garb of clay
And rent in hallowing flame away
The mortal part from the divine—to soar
To the empyreal air! Behold him spring
Blithe in the pride of the unwonted wing,
And the dull matter that confined before
Sinks downward, downward, downward as a
dream!
Olympian hymns receive the escaping soul,
And smiling Hebe, from the ambrosial stream
Fills for a god the bowl!

This is lyric poetry in the most personal, intimate sense of
the word, the expression of heartfelt longings. The image appears again in a letter to Wilhelm von Humboldt in which—
and this is the only place he does so—Schiller writes rapturously of this project. The letter was written in 1795, ten
years before his death. To me this passage is the most remarkable, most revealing, and most moving in all his letters.
He speaks of a kind of poetic composition in which "all mor-
tality would be dissolved, where everything would be pure
light, pure freedom, pure potency—no shadows, no barriers,
nothing of that sort would be visible. I feel literally giddy
when I think of this task, when I conceive the possibility of
accomplishing it. To present a scene in Olympus—that would
be the summit of pleasure! I do not entirely despair of it, if

only my mind could be perfectly free and washed entirely clean of all the refuse of reality; I would then once more summon up all my strength and spiritual resources, even though they were to be entirely consumed on this project."

Truly he was a great, an ever-aspiring soul. When would he have the chance to be "perfectly free and washed entirely clean of all the refuse of reality"? When, here on earth, could his spiritual resources ever have been "rent in hallowing flame away" in order to burn themselves out in such a poem? The idea is utterly transcendental, detached from life, supramundane; it would seem to belong to a spirit already dwelling among the Blessed. In the ten years that remained to Schiller-Hercules he never made a start on the poem of his dreams, for all that it promised him "the summit of pleasure." Yet he conferred a portion of his spiritual resources upon each of his splendid, if earthbound, works, so that all of them carry a glow. But that supramundane dream of pure light and freedom indicates the ultimate goal of his desires. He would, had it been in his power, have thrown off utterly the garb of clay, have become transfigured.

> *Er glänzt vor uns wie ein Komet entschwindend*
> *Unendlich Licht mit seinem Licht verbindend.*

> He shines before us like a comet fleeting,
> Infinitudes of light with his light meeting.

The stanza of which these lines form the solemn conclusion Goethe did not add to his *Epilogue to The Bell* until ten years after his friend's death. But earlier, in the famous lines:

> *Denn hinter ihm in wesenlosem Scheine*
> *Lag, was uns alle bändigt, das Gemeine*

> He left behind, remote and shadowy,
> What fetters all of us: the ordinary

he had reciprocated the selfless act of homage in Schiller's love-poem, *Fortune.*

What is the meaning of *das Gemeine* here? It is not only

commonness and vulgarity. It is the whole natural world, seen from the point of view of the mind and of freedom. It is attachment, dependence and obedience, not will and ethical emancipation. It is what Schiller in his essay called the naïve—and certainly it seems naïve indeed when Goethe, considering in retrospect Schiller's heroic life, warns against the overdoing of the categorical imperative; when he says that Schiller was consumed by intellect, that the idea of freedom literally was the death of him. But though deploring the lack of measure of such an ethical drive, Goethe's Antaean nature stands amazed at its phenomenal results. His wonder became admiration in such recollections as: "Nothing hampered him, nothing restricted him, nothing clipped the wings of his thought. He was as great at the tea table as he would have been in the council of state." Or again: "Schiller was made of very different stuff; in society he always knew how to talk significantly and entrancingly." Whereas he himself was apt to sit all evening without opening his mouth, which naturally produced an oppressive silence, for who would talk if he did not? Conditioned, limited, sensitive to a hundred circumstances, especially the weather (he called himself "a veritable barometer"), without an ounce of faith in freedom of the will, submitting rather to pantheistic necessity, in no way impelled to force anything to come, indulgently waiting for each thing's proper hour, he must have regarded with a kind of horror the person who could admit of himself: "Whatever I am, I have become by an often unnatural tensing of all my powers." He must have felt wonder and a degree of shamefacedness toward the man who could say that he permitted physical ills to exert no dominion upon the freedom and serenity of his mind.

Thus, this splendid friendship was a bond of mutual admiration, a league between intellect and nature. Yet how difficult were its premises, and how patent the profound irony which underlay it—irony on both sides, of course. For what is it but magnificent irony when Schiller warns Goethe

against Kant, his own teacher and idol? Goethe can only be
a Spinozist, he tells him; his beautiful, naïve nature would be
ruined by acceptance of a libertarian philosophy. Intellect, it
would seem, desires nothing less than to convert nature to itself. It warns her against itself. To the sentimental moralist
naïveté appears precious and beautiful. But we cannot help
sensing in this affectionate solicitude a certain tender contempt. Schiller cannot be sufficiently grateful for "the fine
relationship that exists between us." He declares that if he
has surpassed himself in *Wallenstein*, this "is the fruit of our
association." He adds: "For only the continuous intercourse
with a nature objectively so opposed to my own, my own
strong endeavor to achieve that sort of nature, my study of
it and reflection on it, enabled me to move so freely within
my subjective limits." Yet chagrin toward his partner in this
fruitful association lasted until the end of his life. At times it
reached the point of his wishing to break with Goethe. As
late as two years before his death he wrote to Humboldt:
"Goethe has now become a thoroughgoing monk, and lives
in a state of sheer contemplation which, for all that it is not
that of a hermit, does not yield anything that anyone can
see. I can do nothing alone and am often impelled to look
around the world for another place to live. If life were tolerable anywhere else, I would leave."

What about Goethe's part in the relationship? It will always remain a mystery what, at the bottom of his heart, he
thought of Schiller as a writer. "Schiller's conception of writing," Hermann Grimm wrote, "was to Goethe not writing
at all. Schiller's creative method was something alien to Goethe. Schiller looked about for his materials. Then he shaped
and worked them until they felt convenient to his hand."

There are some curious anecdotes on this score. Granted,
their authenticity may be somewhat dubious, yet there is
something basically convincing about them. For example,
we have the testimony of Countess Wagensberg, an admirer
of Goethe whose intelligence and acuteness in other matters

cannot be contested. She speaks, incidentally, of the compunction with which Goethe would enter the realm of sublime ideas where Schiller was so at home. But she comments: "However, it did not seem to me that he admired his friend as a poet, least of all as a dramatic poet. I noticed myself once, when I let drop the question whether Schiller's *Wallenstein* was truly something real and alive, whether its presentation was a work of dramatic genius, that a flush of surprise spread over Goethe's face. His expression seemed to be asking good-humoredly why I should be trying to worm out his most secret convictions. It is therefore my belief that he never gave his friend any hint of what he thought of him as a poet. In general Goethe was far more gentle and kindly toward others, far more sparing of their feelings, than people imagine, and I think there was far less hardness in his character than in Schiller's." The whole story bears the stamp of truth—in spite of the Jovian thunder with which Goethe would answer charges that Schiller was a "thinker and orator," not a poetic genius. He waxes indignant: "Nowadays we hear that our good Schiller was no poet after all, but we know otherwise." And he blusters: "I take the liberty of considering Schiller a true poet, and a great one." But there is an element of doggedness, of loyal determination to fend off criticism, including his own, in that phrase: "I take the liberty."

A certain coarseness in Goethe vanished completely from his language and emotions after his friend's death. One day there was a gathering at Schiller's home, a preliminary conference on the performance of *Mary Stuart*, which he had just completed. The discussion centered chiefly on the fictive scene of Mary's and Elizabeth's meeting in the park of Fotheringay Castle. As he was leaving, Goethe said loudly, right out in the street: "I still wonder how it will strike people when the two whores meet and throw their affairs into each other's faces." Schiller would never have talked so "humorously" about one of his friend's fancies, nor would Goethe ever have been so irreverent after Schiller's passing. Then he could speak of his friend only as the most intelligent, the most purehearted person he had ever met—the only person who he felt ranked with himself. For the survivor the relationship, once the source of a good deal of vexation, was purified more and more into unalloyed appreciation, into those outbursts: "Oh! Do not cause my eyes to swim" or: "I cannot, cannot forget the man." Not that the incompatibility and original strain were forgotten, nor the troubles and sometimes the vexations. Goethe remembered well that "in Schiller's presence art sometimes became a far too serious affair." But he coined a term which excused all the qualities in his late friend's work with which he could not sympathize: "That was not how Schiller did it." It was not how Schiller did it, to provide careful motivations; not how he did it, to proceed instinctively, with a certain lack of consciousness. That great, strange man had to think everything out. It was not at all how he did it, to spin a work of art silently out of his inner self. Rather, he put his hand boldly upon some great subject, observed it, turned it this way and that, looked at it and handled it this way and that. He saw his subjects only from outside, so to speak; that was how he did it, that was his way. His talent was in this sense rather erratic—if the word is taken in the right sense. Proceeding as he did, he could never make up his mind that a given subject was or was not the thing for him, could never really have done with his own work or Goethe's either. He was constantly offering critical suggestions on *Wilhelm Meister*, changing his mind, wanting it given this turn or that, and Goethe had all he could do to maintain himself and his work against these criticisms. Yet he was a great, great, fundamentally strange man, and his like would not be seen again.

Yet, after all, it had been Schiller who had elected to assert himself and defend himself, to be constantly contrasting and formulating what he stood for, in order to match his great friend and rival by distinguishing himself from him—

and it was this which was one of the principal thorns in the relationship. For all his pride, Schiller never lost sight of the fact that his friend's creative powers worked with so much greater ease, so much less coercion, than his own. His admiration and humility were often unlimited. "Goethe's epic poem *Hermann and Dorothea* is the pinnacle of his art, and of our whole modern art. While we others must painfully assemble and test, in order slowly to bring forth something passable, he needs only gently to shake the trees for the finest fruits, ripe and heavy, to fall at his feet." Or: "When Goethe wishes to apply his full powers, I do not measure myself against him. He has far more genius than I, and along with it a far greater wealth of knowledge, a surer sensuousness, and with all this an artistic sense refined and purified by acquaintance with all types of art. This I lack to a degree that amounts to sheer ignorance. If I did not have a few other talents, and if I had not been clever enough to apply these talents and abilities to the field of the drama, I would have made no showing at all beside him in this profession." And he continues: "But what I have done is to shape my own kind of drama according to my talent. That gives me a certain rank in the genre, simply because it is my own." What an amazing sentence! For is not "art" a general heading, in essence totally abstract, which assumes a new and special being in each of its individual expressions and manifestations? Every incarnation of art is a highly personal special case, and the creator often finds it quite difficult to subsume this special case under the grand general notion of art. Every creative production represents a new and in itself highly artistic adaptation of individual predilections and talents to "art." To be exact, art does not exist; there is only the artist and whatever personal arrangement he may make with his work. In that his work is his own, he necessarily achieves "a certain rank."

The passage quoted above is from a letter written in 1789. Seven years later, during his work on *Wallenstein*, he wrote to Wilhelm von Humboldt: "It is true that the road I am

now taking leads me into Goethe's territory, and that I will
have to match myself against him; it is also a foregone conclusion that I shall come out the loser alongside him. But
since something remains to me anyhow which is mine and
which he can never achieve, his superiority detracts nothing
from me or my work, and I hope that the accounts will
square pretty well. Critics will, I promise myself in my most
courageous moments, point out our differences, but will not
rank our genres one below the other, but one alongside the
other as specimens of a higher idealistic species." This was
Schiller's summing-up after that prolonged period of refusal
to match himself in which he did little else but match himself.
It agrees completely with Goethe's: "The Germans are always bickering about who is greater, Schiller or I. They
ought to be glad they have two such boys to bicker about."
But Schiller, dead, became for Goethe what Goethe had
never been to him: sacrosanct. In Goethe's last years his
daughter-in-law, Ottilie, remarked that she found Schiller often boring. Goethe turned his face away and replied: "You
are all far too wretchedly earthbound for him."

We are all called to order by this gesture, this stern re-
proof on the part of Goethe in his old age. We all should take
care that we do not prove too wretchedly earthbound for
the man whom Goethe to his dying day longed to have back
at his side. For it is misguided and wrongheaded to dismiss
his memory, to think that he is out of tune with our times,
outmoded, has nothing more to say to us. That view is itself
outmoded. How keenly I felt this during my recent bout of
rereading his works. He who mastered his own sickness
might well become the physician of our own diseased age,
would it but listen to his voice.

An organism may sicken and waste away because a particular element, some vital substance or vitamin, is lacking in
its body chemistry. Perhaps this indispensable something is
the element of "Schiller" in which our vital economy, the or-

ganism of our society, is so pitifully deficient. So it seemed to me, at any rate, when I reread his "Public Announcement of the *Horen*," that first-class piece of prose in which he dramatizes the timeliness and pertinence of ideas which even in his time must have seemed quite out of date, but which he fashioned into amazing prescripts precisely for the troubles of that time. He speaks in this prospectus of days when "the rumble of imminent war alarms our country; when the internecine struggle of political factions and interests sows this same war within almost every group, so that there is no escape from this ubiquitous demon of political controversy, not in conversation nor in any of the writings of the times." The more, he says, the petty concerns of the present strain, imprison, and subjugate men's minds, the more imperative it becomes to liberate these once more by stimulating interest in those loftier and universal matters which are purely human and superior to temporal influences. The politically divided world, he declares, must be reunited under the banner of truth and beauty. The purpose of his periodical will be to bring tidings of comfort and liberation to the minds and hearts of readers who are alternately outraged and depressed by the events of the day. It will hew to this line in the midst of political tumult, its approach being sometimes light, sometimes serious. Everything tinged by an impure spirit of partisanship will be banished from the journal. But while it will abstain from all references to the present course of world events and the immediate prospects of humanity, it will ask history what may be learned of the past, and philosophy what of the future. It will be a home for the constituents of that ideal of a finer humanity which reason has made manifest, but which life, alas, too often obscures. It will labor quietly for the building of better ideas, purer principles, and nobler ethics, upon which all betterment of the world ultimately depends. "Decency and order, justice and peace, will therefore be the underlying spirit and the watchword of this periodical."

Let us beware of calling such an enterprise feeble aestheticism, or of equating it with what is nowadays called escap-
ism. To contribute to the mind of the nation, its morality and
culture, its spiritual freedom and intellectual level, which
alone renders it capable of understanding that other peoples
born into different historical conditions and living under a
differing ideology, a different social order, are also human
beings—this is not flight from reality. To work for humanity,
to desire decency and order, justice and peace, instead of
mutual recrimination, rank lies, and ferocious hatred—that is
not flight into idle aestheticism. Rather, it is the deepest preoccupation with life; a crusade to cure man of his anxiety and
hatred by freeing his soul. Yet the dream to which Schiller
devoted all his oratorical eloquence and poetic fervor—universality, pure humanity—was viewed by whole generations
as a faded ideal, stale, outmoded, obsolete. What seemed new,
compelling, alive, and true, potent watchwords for the age,
were but certain specific, positive, and nation-centered sentiments. Carlyle, in his otherwise admiring biography of
Schiller, criticized his hero precisely because his heart, like
the Marquis Posa's, "beat for all mankind, for the world and
all coming generations." Schiller had spoken of "us moderns" in contrast to the Greeks and Romans when he declared patriotism an immature concept proper only to an earlier stage of mankind. "It is," he wrote, "a poor and petty aim
to write for a single nation. To the philosophic spirit, such a
limitation is intolerable. Any such spirit cannot confine itself
to so changeable, accidental, and arbitrary an aspect of the
human race. Is not the most important nation a mere fragment? Ardor in its cause is justified only if a step in the history of that nation is also a step in the progress of mankind."

To this form of modernity Carlyle opposes his super-
modernity. "We require," he says, "individuality in our at-
tachments. The sympathy which is expanded over all men
will commonly be found so much attenuated by the process,
that it cannot be effective on any. . . . Universal love of

mankind forms but a precarious and very powerless rule of
conduct. . . . The enthusiasm which pervades [Schiller's
historical works], elevated, strong, enlightened, would have
told better on our hearts had it been confined within a narrower space."

Carlyle's overbearing tone reproduces the dominant note
of a whole era, the era of nationalism. But the language is
that of yesterday. For the historical tides of human thought
ebb and flow, and today we are watching destiny reducing
onetime novelties to obsolescence, reviving ideas that had
been dismissed as over and done with, revealing them as the
ideas of our time, conferring a burning, vital contemporane-
ity upon them, making them, as never before, a matter of life
and death. Where do we stand today? The idea of nationalism, the idea of a "narrower space," already belongs to the
past. It can help us no longer—this we all feel—to solve any
political, economic, or intellectual problems. Universality is
the demand of the hour and of our anxious souls. The word
"humanity," the idea of the honor of mankind and of the
widest possible sympathy, has long since ceased to be a
"powerless rule of conduct" which "attenuates" our emotions. This very all-embracing feeling is what we need, need
all too bitterly; and unless mankind as a whole comes to its
senses and remembers its honor, the mystery of its dignity, it
is lost, not only morally but physically as well.

The past half-century has witnessed a regression of humanity, a chilling atrophy of culture, a frightening decrease
in civility, decency, sense of justice, loyalty, and faith, and
of the most elementary trustworthiness. Two world wars,
breeding brutality and rapacity, have catastrophically low-
ered the intellectual and moral level (the two are inseparable) and left behind a state of disorder which is a poor safe-
guard against the plunge into a third war that would end
everything. Rage and fear, unreasoning hatred, panicky terror, and a wild lust for persecution ride mankind. The human race exults in the conquest of space for the establish-

ment of strategic bases in it, and counterfeits the energy of
the sun for the criminal purpose of manufacturing weapons
of annihilation.

> *Find' ich so den Menschen wieder,*
> *Dem wir unser Bild geliehn,*
> *Dessen schöngestalte Glieder*
> *Droben in Olympus blühn?*
> *Gaben wir ihm zum Besitze*
> *Nicht der Erde Götterschoß,*
> *Und auf seinem Königsitze*
> *Schweift er elend, heimatlos?*

> Can this, then, be man indeed,
> Fashioned on our godlike lines?
> This the well-appointed breed
> Upon which Olympus shines?
> Did he not from us receive
> Earth for his appointed home?
> Is this all he can achieve—
> Desolate, abroad to roam?

This is the lament of Ceres in *The Eleusinian Festival.* It is
Schiller's voice. Heedless of his call to "labor quietly for the
building of better ideas, purer principles, and nobler ethics,
upon which all betterment of the world ultimately depends,"
a human race besotted with idiocies, a race gone to seed,
bawling out the latest world records in technology and
sports, staggers toward a doom that is no longer entirely un-
wanted.

When the hundredth anniversary of Schiller's birth was
celebrated in November 1859, a wave of enthusiasm united
all of Germany. This was truly the case, we are told; and
what an astounding sight it was: the eternally disunited German people for once forming a close-knit body to honor
their poet. It was a national celebration. Let ours be one
also. In the face of a political enormity, let divided Germany
feel united in his name. That is all very well. But in these

present times of ours, let us give another, greater symbolic meaning to our memorial celebration. May it stand under the sign of universal sympathy, true to the spirit of his own noble-minded greatness, which called for an eternal covenant of man with the earth that gave him birth. May something of his heroic will enter into us through this celebration of his interment and resurrection; some small part of his will to achieve beauty, truth, and goodness, moral excellence, inner freedom, art, love, peace, and man's saving reverence for himself.

Translated by Richard and Clara Winston

(*A Weary Hour*, a short story by Thomas Mann (1905), whose protagonist is Schiller, is reprinted in the Appendix, p. 204.)

FANTASY ON GOETHE

THE CHILD whom an eighteen-year-old mother brought into the world with great travail on August 28, 1749, just as the clock struck noon, was blue and looked lifeless. It seemed not to respond to the light that flooded into the Frankfurt burgher's home, and seemed prepared to go directly from the maternal womb to a little grave, as if it were unwilling to set out upon a path of life which was to carry it so far, to be so richly fruitful, so blessed with fulfillments, so glorious an example. Some time passed before the grandmother, standing behind the bed, could call out to the sighing mother: "Elisabeth, he is living!" It was the cry of a woman to a woman, of animal joy, a homely, household exclamation —that was all. And yet it should have been shouted to the world, to all humanity. Even today, two centuries later, it holds its full measure of gladness, and will do so through all times to come. As long as life and love exist upon this earth, as long as life shall love itself and not weary of its sweet pangs, as long as life does not turn in ennui away from itself, this woman's cry which was unwittingly so great an annunciation will remain and resound: "He is living!"

The human soul delivered so woefully and well-nigh smothered from the dark womb was predestined to a tremendous reach of life. He was fated to set up a new canon of life's potentialities, to exhibit enormous powers of growth and rejuvenation, to satisfy to the full all that can be demanded of a man, and to attain a majesty before which kings and nations bowed. He became a phenomenon whose natural origins he himself once made the object of earnest study. Eighty-three years had passed since that summer's noon of his birth. Great gobs of history had meanwhile rolled ponderously by, oppressing his mind: the Seven Years' War, the American War of Independence, the French Revolution, the rise and fall of Napoleon, the dissolution of the Holy Roman Empire, the dawn of the nineteenth century with its transformations of the very air and physiognomy of the world, the onset of the bourgeois age, the machine age, the July Revolution. The old man who had survived it all, upright and snow-white of hair, strange rings of age around his pupils lending a birdlike, darting quality to his brown, close-set eyes, stood at the lectern of his intentionally uncomfortable study at Weimar—in the house which man's impulse to venerate has long since made a place of pilgrimage—stood at his desk and wrote his last letter to an old friend. His eyes transfixed with reveries and lucid meditation, he wrote to Wilhelm von Humboldt, the philologist and statesman, in Berlin:

". . . The best genius is the one which absorbs everything, which is capable of appropriating everything without detriment to its underlying disposition, which we call character. Rather, what comes from outside should improve it and as far as possible add to its potentialities. . . . By training, instruction, reflection, success, failure, stimulus, obstacles, and more and more reflection, man's faculties, in their untrammeled, unconscious activity, unite acquired with innate traits, producing a unity which astounds the world. Faithfully yours, J. W. v. Goethe."

What magnificent naïveté, what naïve magnificence, in this contemplation of the self! There is something at once childlike and daemonic, at once charming and formidable about it. Seventeen years earlier he had written a poem summing up his life in terms just as stunning and touching as that phrase "astounds the world." At that time he had fallen in love with a newly married young woman, Marianne von Willemer, the Suleika of the *Westöstlicher Divan*. If this affair was not commenced for the purposes of art, it was at least artistically fruitful—nor was it by any means his final passion. That overwhelmed him at the age of seventy-four when His Excellency, world-famous poet and the highest ranking minister of the Grand Duchy of Saxe-Weimar, once more became a ballroom lion and Lothario at Marienbad. He flirted and wooed, billed and cooed, and insisted that he wanted to marry a seventeen-year-old chit of a girl. Nothing came of it, since his family was solidly opposed and the girl herself was not altogether taken with the idea—although she never did marry anyone else. But to return to the poem written at sixty-six—Goethe, head over heels in love with Marianne von Willemer and his feelings sentimentally reciprocated under the eyes of her obliging husband, wrote these lines:

> *Nur dies Herz, es ist von Dauer,*
> *Schwillt in jugendlichstem Flor,*
> *Unter Schnee und Nebelschauer*
> *Rast ein Ätna dir hervor.*

> *Du beschämst wie Morgenröte*
> *Jener Gipfel ernste Wand*
> *Und noch einmal fühlet Hatem*
> *Frühlingshauch und Sommerbrand.*

> This heart only never cowers,
> Ever budding like the spring,
> Under snows and misty showers,
> Aetna's fires hiss and sing.

> Dawn is coming still, though later,
> To the mountain's somber spire,
> And he still responds, our Hatem,
> To spring's fragrance, summer's fire.

Aetna is a bit of poetic license. As I know him, his heart never raged like a volcano for any woman; he held no brief for vulcanism of any sort—not even for it as a scientific theory. But *jener Gipfel ernste Wand*—what authority lies in this calm, truthful, unconceited, and wholly sublime evaluation of himself. To say of oneself, to be justified in saying of oneself: I resemble a mighty, towering massif, awesome, inaccessible, forbidding in its somberness, but tenderly illumined by the sweet dawn which does not shrink from its fierce grandeur, which is the first to kiss it, transfigure it, bring a blush to its craggy features.

For the non-German reader a curiosity of the rhyme scheme must be pointed out. The structure of the poem calls for a rhyme to the word *Morgenröte* in the third line of the stanza. The Oriental name Hatem, which is fobbed off on the reader's ear, does not fit at all. Involuntarily, with amusement and a bit of dismay, the ear completes the coyly concealed rhyme as it is intended to do.* The real name is Goethe— that curious, now vanished surname of a family which had produced many feeble and inconsequential persons until, through this one latecomer possessed of an incomparable capacity for uniting acquired with innate traits, it has become a palladium for humanity, a name embracing whole worlds of art, wisdom, culture, civilization, has passed through an evolution of meaning reminiscent of the transformations in the name of Caesar. *Goethe*—the barbarian element (for the nomen probably comes from "Goth") has been poetically refined by the flutelike mutation of the vowel. And this is the name which its owner, in deep-felt earnestness, rhymes with one of the loveliest phenomena of the sensual world: *Morgenröte*, the flush of dawn.

We have here a kind of splendid narcissism, a contentment with self far too serious and far too concerned to the very end with self-perfection, heightening, and distillation of personal endowment, for a petty-minded word like "vanity" to be applicable. Here is that profound delight in the self and its growth to which we owe *Poetry and Truth*, the best, at any rate the most charming autobiography the world has seen—

---

* We have attempted to render this with a rhyme (*later*) which corresponds to the efforts of English-speaking persons to pronounce Goethe's name.—TRANSLATORS' NOTE.

essentially a novel in the first person which informs us, in the most wonderfully winning tone, how a genius is formed, how luck and merit are indissolubly linked by an unknown decree of grace and how a personality grows and flourishes under the sun of a higher dispensation. Personality! Goethe called it "the supreme bliss of mortal man"—but what it really is, in what its inner nature consists, wherein its mystery lies—for there is a mystery about it—not even he ever explained. For that matter, for all his love for the telling word, for the word that strikes to the heart of life, he never thought that everything must be explained. Certainly this phenomenon known as "personality" takes us beyond the sphere of purely intellectual, rational, analyzable matters into the realm of nature, where dwell those elemental and daemonic things which "astound the world" without being amenable to further elucidation.

The above-mentioned Wilhelm von Humboldt, a singularly intelligent person, commented a few days after Goethe's death on how remarkable it was that unconsciously, virtually without meaning to, by his mere existence, Goethe had exercised such enormous influence. "This is separate from his creative work as a thinker and writer," Humboldt wrote; "it is due to his great and unique personality." Here we see that this word is a mere linguistic stopgap for something that language cannot cope with, for an emanation whose sources are not intellectual but vitalistic. Personality, exerting the ultimate in fascination and magnetism, must be the effect of a special vitality peculiarly compounded of strength and frailty, concentrated and powerful but not crude or simple, whose production is one of the dark creative secrets of nature's laboratory.

So a genetic stream runs on through the centuries of German life, runs casually, ordinary and unnoticed. Everything indicates that Nature has no special end in mind for it. Yet it terminates in the one unique personality. For, as he will make his Iphigenia say:

Denn es erzeugt nicht gleich
Ein Haus den Halbgott, noch das Ungeheuer;
Erst eine Reihe Böser oder Guter
Bringt endlich das Entsetzen, bringt die Freude
Der Welt hervor.

> For seldom does a stock produce at once
> A monster or a demigod; it takes a line
> Of good or evil men to first usher in
> The blessing or the terror of the world.

The demigod or the monster—the latter being the subhuman. He conceives the two together, takes the one for the other, and knows that there must be some horror amid blessings, some of the monster in the demigod. In unemotional prose he says: "If families persist for a long time it happens that before they die out one individual appears who comprehends in himself the traits of all his ancestors, uniting and completely expressing all their previously isolated and latent characteristics." Here, neatly formulated and set down as a scientific theory, is the considered summary of his deductions from his own far from normal existence. But what was the evolutionary process? How did the precipitation come about? In a highly surreptitious, highly unostentatious way. The clans of artisans, blacksmiths, and butchers cross and beget. The wandering journeyman from the neighboring principality follows the old custom and marries the master's daughter; the count's scullery maid is wed to the official surveyor or educated administrator—a potpourri of assorted life cradled between birth and death which does not seem to amount to much. Gradually an element of property and culture, urban status and patricianism, enters in, and eventually the dignity of a chief magistrate—when the Lindheimers intermarry with the Textors, a family that had immigrated to Frankfurt from South Germany, and the latter with the Goethes, who sprang from a more northern region between the Thuringian forest and the Harz Mountains.

The Lindheimers' ancestral home lay close to the ancient Roman *limes*, where the blood of Romans and barbarians had mingled from time immemorial. Theirs was, I think, the best, healthiest, and most felicitous ingredient in the great poet's nature. His mother's mother, a Lindheimer married to a Textor, had been a plain, sturdy, dark-complexioned woman of docile femininity. From her, if we may judge by pictures, he inherited his forehead, the shape of his head and mouth, the Italianate eyes, and the Mediterranean complexion. From this side of the family, too, there certainly came the classical elements in his nature, the desire for form and clarity, wit, irony, and grace. From her, too, came his peculiar aloofness from Teutonism, which often found vent in critical disgust and wrath. Yet at the same time the German component was strong in him, assuming a blunt, stoutly traditional national character, a saltiness stemming straight from Hans Sachs and Luther. We may say that never has such unemotional and authoritative criticism of the Germanic spirit come from a more Germanic temperament, that never was there a more German anti-barbarism.

The other elements in the family combination that was destined to produce the demigod were not, biologically speaking, especially promising. His paternal grandfather, Friedrich Georg Goethe, was a tailor who obviously went somewhat off his rocker in his old age. Twice married, he had eleven children, most of whom died in infancy. Of the three who survived him, the eldest was indubitably mentally ill, and died insane at the age of forty-three. The poet's father, Johann Kaspar, was the tenth of the eleven, a late-born child of parents well on in years. He showed the effects. A jurist who had purchased the title of Imperial Councillor, he was an oddly testy person, quick to take offense, a morose eccentric who did not practice his profession, an ardent collector, dreary pedant, and querulous hypochrondriac who complained about every draft which disturbed his painful routine. Elisabeth, the cheerful daughter of the chief magis-

trate and of Grandmother Lindheimer, was wedded to him
when she was only seventeen, half his age. That was a misfortune for her, since she spent her best years nursing a decrepit tyrant. Her father, Johann Wolfgang Textor, must
also have been a "blithe spirit"—as Goethe called his mother
—at least in his youth. That is to say, he was a man about
town and reckless petticoat-chaser who was sometimes
caught shamefully *in flagrante* by irate husbands. Yet he was
also—a strange mixture—a seer who had the gift of prophecy.
In his old age (he lived to be eighty) he grew to be as grave,
silent, stern, and dignified as he had been uproarious in his
youth. His last years were spent in a wheelchair, a senile
invalid.

Elisabeth, the Imperial Councillor's wife, had six confine-
ments, but in four of them she labored only for death. After
a few days each of the children promptly went back into the
darkness from which it had come, and only one sister, along
with Wolfgang, survived infancy. This was Cornelia, an un-
happily bitter girl who suffered from neurotic acne. Frigid,
epicene, a stranger on earth, destined "rather to be an abbess
than a wife," she nevertheless tried marriage, only to die
wretchedly in childbed, the very prospect of which had filled
her with horror. Wolfgang alone lived on, lived for all six,
we might say, although he did not always possess the vitality
that the others had lacked and which he had with metaphysical avarice grasped for himself.

One of his grandsons, who were but shadows of men, used
to say in melancholic self-mockery: "What do you expect;
my grandfather was a man of might, but I am only a mite of
a man." But the man of might was not invulnerable. Tuberculosis, latent for decades, seems to have run through his
whole life. As a student in Leipzig, where he lived with great
irregularity, either roistering from high spirits or neglecting
himself from romantic despondency, he put his health to a
severe trial. He suffered a hemorrhage and returned home a
broken young man, having failed completely in his studies, to

his bitterly disappointed parents. And in his eighty-first year, after the death of his unfortunate son, he again experienced a severe hemorrhage. Incredible to relate, at that age he lost five pounds of blood—for there was also a blood-letting prescribed by his physicians—and nevertheless recovered. Then, compensating by "determination and character" for the deficiencies of "spontaneously active nature," he proceeded to complete the fourth act of *Faust*.

Recovered from the lingering illness which had kept him hovering on the brink of the grave, young Goethe went to Strassburg to continue his studies at law. There, from his twentieth to his twenty-third year, he diverted himself with dabblings into esoteric science, poetry, and aesthetics. At Wetzlar he ostensibly practiced as "Licentiate" (or Doctor) of Law at the Imperial Supreme Court. But in reality he was doing nothing but loving, suffering, cultivating his enthusiasms, loafing, and giving himself time for inner growth. This rearing, kicking, thoroughbred colt, this embryo genius, must simultaneously have irritated and fascinated people of every age and disposition—arousing vexed laughter by a hundred affectations in dress and manners, by intolerable "presumption" and fantastic callowness; and winning friends by the splendor of his youth, his radiant talent, an almost palpable electric charge of vitality, coupled with an indescribable naïveté and the good nature of a dear lad somewhat spoiled by himself and others, but full of the best intentions.

He was very handsome at that time, fond of children and the common people, which is to say fond of nature. At the same time he was "extremely frivolous and impudent as a sparrow"—so Herder characterized him—"a young coxcomb impatiently strutting about." That is, he was so whenever he did not happen to be drooping with a lover's melancholy or unassuageable *Weltschmerz*, in which case he would try stabbing a knife a little deeper each day into his flesh near his heart. "I do not know what attractiveness I must have for

people," he wrote of himself. "So many of them like me."
This "attractiveness" must at any rate have been at its height
when at the age of twenty-six Goethe, already famous as the
author of glorious lyrics, of *Götz von Berlichingen*, of *Werther*, and of a number of incredibly vigorous and gripping
fragments of a poem on Faust, made his entry into Weimar
as the young Duke's new favorite. Supposedly he came for
only a brief visit; in reality he was destined to spend his life
there. Wieland, the tutor of the young princes of Weimar
and already a man of forty-two, was spokesman of the general enthusiasm when he wrote, shortly after the arrival of
the guest from Frankfurt: "Since this morning my soul is as
full of Goethe as a dewdrop of the morning sun." And he
had resorted to verse in order to describe the young man
"with a pair of jet-black eyes":

Zaubernden Augen voll Götterblicken,
Gleich mächtig zu töten und zu entzücken,
So trat er unter uns, herrlich und hehr,
Ein echter Geisterkönig daher!
So hat sich nie in Gottes Welt
Ein Menschensohn uns dargestellt,
Der alle Güte und alle Gewalt
Der Menschheit so in sich vereinigt!

Der unzerdrückt von ihrer Last
So mächtig alle Natur umfaßt,
So tief in jedes Wesen sich gräbt,
Und doch so innig im Ganzen lebt!
Das lass' mir einen Zaubrer sein!
Was macht er nicht aus unsern Seelen?
Wer kann so lieblich ängsten und quälen?
Wer aus der Seelen innersten Tiefen
Mit solch entzückendem Ungestüm
Gefühle erwecken, die ohne ihn
Uns selbst verborgen im Dunkeln schliefen? . . .

Fascination and divinity
Lie in his eyes, which all at once may be
Deadly or sweet, may praise or blame.
A prince of thought among us—so he came,
And on all God's earth
Never was there a man of greater worth.
He closes in himself all of man's pity
And all the violence of humanity.
He clasps nature whole, and still stands straight,
Uncrushed by all that weight.
He burrows into every living soul
And still comprehends the whole.
What a spellbinder is this!
How he makes us dance to his tune,
Charms us while he makes us groan.
Into our hearts the man has bored
And with amiable impertinences
Stirred up feelings we'd ignored,
Roused up all our slumbering senses. . . .

From this effusive tribute we can measure the vital magnetism, the rays of sheer intellectual vitality, which must have
streamed from this man after he had left the colt-and-sparrow
stage behind him and already had some presentiment of the
majestic mission awaiting him on this earth. He indulged the
madcap wildness of his youth only to keep up with his young
sovereign, who loved him, while at the same time surrepti-
tiously and successfully leading him in the direction of seriousness, hard work, and goodness.

His move to Weimar and entry into government service,
or, rather, direction of the administration of a small state,
seemed outwardly a matter of pure chance. But it was chance
that conformed to an inward plan of life, was brought his
way through what Goethe called "guidance from above."
For never were a poet's life and work more closely inter-
twined, more inseparably allied. Thus, his work was pure ex-

perience, expression, lyrical confession, which, for all that
its form was predestined, drew heavily upon the life for certain of its phases.

At Karlsruhe two noblemen who admired Goethe, the
Counts Stolberg, had introduced him to Crown Prince Karl
August. At this time the poet was engaged to Lili Schöne-
mann, the charming daughter of a wealthy Frankfurt
burgher. He had entered upon the engagement out of love or
infatuation, but the happy prospective bridegroom was
strangely unhappy in the face of the folly he was about to
commit. Something within him sensed that it would impede
his work, with the result that he was mysteriously tormented
by pangs of conscience over the impending commitment to
respectable married life. This conscience of his urged flight,
as it had done several times before, and his joining the enthusiastic young noblemen on a trip to Switzerland was just
such an escape. "I must be off into the free world!" a voice
cried within him—he promptly recorded it on paper. The
voice that cried along with him, or used him as its instrument, belonged to the protagonist of his favorite work, the
work which was to occupy his life—at that time still lingering in a phase of highly immature youthful charm, but destined to undergo a tremendous process of aging and matur-
ing. It was the voice of Faust, crying to be led into active
life, into the great world. Among other things, he had to be
brought to a ducal court. And Goethe himself contrived to
reach a ducal court.

Karl August of Saxe-Weimar, says his biographer, fell in
love twice on that trip to Switzerland: with the beautiful
Princess Luise of Hesse-Darmstadt, his betrothed, and with
Dr. Goethe. When he met Goethe again in Frankfurt, some
time afterward, he was the reigning Duke and had just been
married. He brought the pair of them home together, his
new wife and his favorite. With Goethe for companion, he
then inaugurated a round of sovereign and spirited amuse-
ments in his tiny capital and in the villages, hunting-ground,

and parks roundabout. At the same time he gave his friend his full confidence and heaped honors and authority upon him—much to the dismay of his worthy seasoned councillors, who thought that a completely inexperienced so-called "original genius," this vagrant Frankfurt lawyer and poet, deserved no such position.

Karl August forcefully disagreed. "You will see for yourself," he wrote to Von Fritsch, his grumbling, protesting Prime Minister, who had threatened to resign, "that a man such as this would never endure the dull and mechanical work in some local office which would be incumbent upon him if he started at the bottom. Not to use a man of genius where he can employ his extraordinary talents would be tantamount to misusing him." Whereupon Karl August appointed his twenty-seven-year-old friend Privy Legation Councillor, with a seat and vote in the Cabinet and a salary of twelve hundred thalers annually. Six years later he raised him to Acting Privy Councillor, added the titles of Minister and Excellency, and the same year induced the Emperor to grant him hereditary nobility—which did not make any special impression upon Goethe since "we Frankfurt patricians have always considered ourselves equals of the nobility." We must not imagine that he ever regarded his elevation—which is so strongly reminiscent of Joseph's raising up by Pharaoh —as in the least overwhelming, or as the fulfillment of a dream. "I have never known a person more presumptuous than myself," he remarks in a little self-analysis, "and that I say this proves the statement. I never thought anything had to be attained; I always felt that I already had it. A crown could have been placed upon my head, and I would have thought: this is perfectly normal. . . . But when I had grasped something beyond my powers, I always worked to master it; when I received something beyond my merits, I always tried to deserve it. In this I differed from the true madman."

These are not the words of an ambitious man, or a complacent one. Rather, he speaks as one whom nature has favored, who has already received everything without effort, but who is a serious soul and willing to work to deserve what is already his. Commenting on a portrait of him painted in his old age, someone said to him that this was obviously a man who had suffered much. The matter ought to be phrased in rather more active terms, Goethe replied; it would be more correct to say: "Here is a man who worked his head off."

And truly he did work his head off as minister, favorite, and "Second in the Realm," as he once called himself—surely making some allusion to Joseph. He worked as the Duke's mentor, sometimes restraining him and sometimes leading him forward, and as the soul of the Weimar government. For ten years, from the time his boundlessly trustful sovereign entrusted the presidency of the Chamber to him, he was jack-of-all-trades in the little state, "the marrow of things," as someone said of him in mockery or amazement. Meanwhile, his literary reputation almost faded, and he himself attempted to repress his greatest gift, his natural vocation. "I withdraw as much of the water as possible from these fountains and cascades," he wrote, "and divert it to mills and irrigation ditches." In this case, the mills and irrigation ditches were ex-cise taxes, regulations for cloth-manufactures, levies of troops, building of canals and roads, poorhouses, mines and quarries, finances, and a hundred other things. In a veritable passion for self-conquest he issued orders to himself, such as: "Iron patience. Stony endurance!" He achieved a good deal by way of order and thrift in a rather run-down little eighteenth-century state. But in the end he came to the con-clusion: "How much better for me if I could turn my mind from the conflicts of politics to the sciences and arts for which I was born. With what effort I have torn myself away from Aristotle to devote myself to leases and pasturage rights. Properly speaking, I was made for private life, and do not understand how fate has contrived to thrust me into gov-ernment administration and a princely family." His final summary was: "Whoever becomes involved in administration without being a reigning sovereign must be either a philistine, a scoundrel, or a fool."

There is a remarkable saying of his which runs: "Whether a man expresses his genius in science or in war and government, or in a song, it is all the same; all that matters is that the idea, the *aperçu,* the act is alive and capable of surviving."

This is directed against his age's narrowly aesthetic conception of genius; these are the words of a man who will not be content with little, of an integral human being who knows that a great writer primarily possesses the quality of greatness—and is a writer only secondarily. And yet it turned out that to relegate one's true activity to one side, to see it as interchangeable with any other, as "only a parable," was to carry the principle too far. Grief and illness follow when Pegasus is forced to turn the mill. Goethe grieved and fell ill; he ceased to speak freely, wilted physically—and fled, once more fled head over heels. One cause of his flight was a love affair pitched on so ethereal a plane as to be altogether enervating: his relationship with a lady of the court, Frau von Stein. This was a curiously ecstatic, in some respects quite obscure, and not altogether wholesome passion which in a perplexing manner dominated a whole decade of his life —a surprisingly protracted, half-mystical seizure. Had it lasted longer, had he not run away from it, it would certainly have gravely impaired his nature, his bond with life, the elements in himself which he symbolized in the Earth Spirit in *Faust.* And without this earthiness his writing was exposed to the dangers of pallid dilution and emasculation.

Not that this strange passion, which probably never developed into a physical relationship, had been altogether unfruitful. *Iphigenia, Tasso,* even Mignon's songs of longing sprang from it. And yet when he says that the principal object of his Italian journey—this flight carried out in such haste and secrecy—was "to cure him of the physical and moral ills which tormented him in Germany," we may con-

nect the name of Charlotte von Stein with these ills, this torment, and this thirst for a cure, for all that he chivalrously
refrained from mentioning her.

So he went off to Italy on a furlough from public affairs
lasting a full two years. He lived under a classic sky, in the
midst of a southern people, devoting himself to contemplation of antiquity and great art. This was for him an educational experience which went far beyond what the polite
court-of-love adoration at Weimar could ever have given
him. We find it difficult to grasp the full meaning and nature
of his experience, to understand his inner upheaval and sense
of renewal, or the emotions that prompted his incessant ex-
clamations over his happiness and new-won freedom. "I
count it a second birthday, a true rebirth, from the day I entered Rome." Or: "A new youth, a second youth, a new
man, a new life." Or: "I think I have been changed to the
very marrow of my bones." Such cries of joy he addressed
to many of his correspondents, including Charlotte von
Stein, whom he had left without a parting word. Even the
literary historians and specialists in Goethe know less about
the true meaning of this renascence than they pretend. He
seems to have foreseen it, desired it, felt it to be vitally necessary, for it began immediately after his departure. The essence of it seems to have been a reintegration of his personality, of the tendencies within himself which pulled him two
ways: toward nature and the intellect, toward science and
art, toward sensuality and morality. To use his own words,
he had the need to be "definite, vital, coherent." Wholeness
was what he sought, and the word was on his lips constantly
at this period. "Natural history, art, manners, etc.—everything is becoming amalgamated in me. . . . I feel the sum
of my forces compacting." Everything compacted in his
study of classical antiquity, which he contemplated not from
the point of view of an aesthete but as a magnificent natural
growth. Now he developed a far more vigorous attitude toward antiquity, an attitude at once loftier and cruder. Under

the aegis of Charlotte von Stein he had been formally con-
verted to classicism, or rather classicisticism; *Iphigenia* and
Tasso were products of this conversion.

This classicistic tendency had stood for culture, restraint,
morality, the influence of feminine soulfulness; fundamentally it had been something extremely anti-pagan. But the
result of his stay in Italy was the coalescence and union of
the concepts of "antiquity" and "nature." In Italy, as he said
later, "the hitherto cribbed and intimidated child of nature
drank in the air freely."

The experience with pagan naïveté, with the naturalness of
life among a southern people, was enormously important to
him. It meant happiness and wholeness. "Incidentally," he
writes, "I have met happy people who are that solely because they are whole. . . . This I want too and must now attain. . . . I would rather be dead than again undergo life as
I have lived it these past years." It is almost incredible that
he should say this to, of all persons, Frau von Stein. She
could not help reading between the lines his desire to break
with her. But, then, every word he wrote was really directed
against her and her ethereal sphere. "My existence has now
acquired ballast which gives it the necessary weight; I no
longer fear the ghosts which used to disport with me." What
is the opposite of ghostliness? Substantiality. "Anyone who
seriously looks around here, and has eyes to see, cannot help
becoming substantial; he must grasp as a vital principle the
concept of substantiality." His conception of love, too, became "substantial," pagan, classic, naïve, and "whole." In
love, to quote the *Roman Elegies*, "Desire followed the look,
enjoyment followed desire." In 1795 his soulful Charlotte
had to read that in print. She must have raised her eyes to
Heaven.

We can fairly well postulate and reconstruct the other experiences which contributed to that epoch-making solidifica-
tion, that toughening of his personality. There was the contact with the Mediterranean temper, with which in some

mysterious way he had a blood kinship. There was his immersion in a non-German world, which had a liberating and beneficent effect upon him. There was the environment of historic grandeur, which appealed to his instinct for greatness. The fact is Italy made a whole man out of this urbane genius, this cultivated titan, this European German who turned to the world a distinctly German, to his own nation a European, face.

Thus the thirty-nine-year-old poet returned to Weimar, with assurances from the Duke that henceforth he would have only the honors but none of the duties attached to his high position in the state. That is to say, Goethe would be asked only to exercise a little supervision over the theater and educational institutions, but otherwise would be free to devote himself to his work. He was a remarkable person, this minuscule pharaoh who had such instinct and insight into the uniqueness of his Joseph—he was himself, among the princes of Germany, a thoroughly unique phenomenon entitled to our eternal respect. One order of his makes a very pretty detail in the mosaic of their relationships: that Goethe, if he wished to attend a session of the Cabinet or the Chamber, should have the right to sit in the chair reserved for the Duke. And this selfsame Goethe, in his capacity of administrator, had reduced the Duke's standing army by half—taking away 290 of his 600 soldiers.

He returned to a world of petty provincials, crude or with intellectual pretensions, narrow-minded, primly gossipy, prudish, and constricted of horizon. He returned a different person from the man who had fled. He was now firm, complete, experienced, and at peace with himself, his heart filled with feelings of aloofness. Henceforth he was to be basically solitary. To open his heart, to communicate with others, had now become difficult for him. People thought that he either pretended to be banally conventional or was being deliberately singular, was putting on airs. They could not make him out. And he, for his part, was unable to return to his free-

and-easy basis with old friends. Everyone felt the chill he exuded, and after a gathering in his home at which he tried to ease the tension by showing sketches, someone reported: "All of us felt extremely uncomfortable." His kindness had become condescension, reserved politeness. Thus, Schiller, who during his first winter in Weimar was scarcely noticed by Goethe, set down his impressions of the other man: "He has a gift for fascinating people and of being amiable to them with small as well as large attentions, but he manages to keep himself free of attachment all the while. He makes his existence pleasantly known, but only as would a god, without giving anything of himself." Here Schiller speaks with the heightened penetration of an insulted soul.

We have also the testimony of Mme Karoline Herder, wife of the famous preacher, philosopher of art, and collector of folk songs, who had been Goethe's mentor in Strassburg and whom he had in the course of time brought to Weimar as "superintendent general" of the church. She commented: "He no longer wants to be anything to his friends. He is no longer adjusted to Weimar." She said, too, taking the characteristic Weimar tone: "Oh, if only he could put a little heart into his creations, and if only we did not have to see a kind of indecency in all of them, or, as he himself is fond of calling it, the intimate manner." Excellent Karoline! He himself informs Frau von Stein: "My virtues are growing, but my virtue diminishing." It cannot be put more pithily or more cuttingly. Italy, antiquity, intercourse with great art had not made him any more soulful. To the perplexing elements in his nature had been added a scandalous touch of willful sensuality, a sensuality undeterred by Christian conscience, full of lordly defiance to Christian morality and its social simperings. He had adopted a pagan attitude which induced his cultivated acquaintances—and how cultivated they all were!—to give him the horrified nickname of "Priapus."

It was at this time that he reduced to despair his forsaken

Iphigenia and Princess d'Este, Frau von Stein, and utterly outraged all persons of standing and morality—by taking to his bed a pretty and completely uneducated little flower-girl, *un bel pezzo di carne*, Christiane Vulpius by name. It was a liaison of challenging libertinage which he did not legalize until many years later. Society never forgave him or her for it. He had several children by her, of whom only one, August, survived to middle age—a joy neither to himself nor to his father, for he was an ill-starred creature, drunken and dissolute, intemperate, brutal, and weak, a poor, desperate soul from the start.

His father's durable physique passed through phases which have been preserved for us in paintings, sketches, silhouettes, and the descriptions of contemporaries. In his youth he had resembled a foppish Apollo or, rather, a Hermes (aside from somewhat too short legs). But by the beginning of the new century, which he was to inhabit for a full generation, his body assumed that clumsy corpulence which had already begun to develop during his stay in Italy. For many years his fundamentally handsome face displayed a sullen fatness, with drooping jowls. In old age, however, his appearance once again approached that of his youth, except that the Apollo or Hermes had been transformed into a Jupiter emanating the maximum of majesty, half king and half father, as Grillparzer said. His was a wonderful head with a magnificent craggy brow. He had lost little of his hair, and kept it carefully curled and lightly powdered. His commanding black eyes flashed with intellectual energy whenever they did not happen to be muted and veiled by fatigue. His clothing was exceedingly distinguished and select, though somewhat old-fashioned in style. Moreover, with advancing age the stiffness, the dignified demeanor which had characterized him even as a youth, emerged more and more. A formality bordering on crotchetiness, a deliberate conventionality, often held his conversation to the level of any cultivated Cabinet minister, so that a good many worshipful visitors to the author of *Werther and Wilhelm Meister* departed from him profoundly sobered, chilled, and disillusioned. His paternal heritage from old Johann Kaspar made a ghostly reappearance in his rigid pedantry and pettifogging tidiness, and in his eccentric collecting mania and multifarious interests. There is no doubt that he was conscious of this reversion—on a far higher plane; that he recognized with fantastic serenity the old man in himself, and smiled in secret as he sublimated the image of his father.

At that time, when he was between the ages of seventy and eighty, he had long since ceased to be merely the author of *Werther*, *Faust*, and other great works. He had already become an almost mythical figure, the foremost representative of Occidental culture, and could view himself in historic terms. He was a towering figure of highest intellectual stature, whom people from all the countries of Europe and even from across the ocean approached with reverence and often with shaking knees. Visitors who wore spectacles were in the habit of depositing these in the anteroom, since it was well known that he hated to look into glittering glasses. He would thoroughly interrogate travelers who had seen anything, had anything to tell, saying: "Stop, let us linger on this point," and asking for precise information. For he wanted to know everything, to be the repository of all the knowledge others happened to possess. Knowledge, after all, was safest with him. If a visitor was moderately interesting and could contribute something useful to his universalism, he would be invited to lunch—and treated to excellent food and drink while he was further quizzed. He might then be permitted to see one or another of the collections with which the fine house on the Frauenplan, the Duke's gift to Goethe, was crammed: engravings, medallions, minerals, precious antiques. "I possess the coins of all the popes from the fifteenth century to the present day," the old man was wont to say. "They are of great interest for the history of art. I know all the engravers. Greek coinage of Alexander's time and earlier has not yet

been equaled." This was only one small province of the empire of knowledge he ruled and whose symbols he kept
clustered about him in portfolios, chests, and glass cases.

He was one of the most comprehensive, many-sided dilet-
tantes that ever lived, an amateur in everything. Nor was he
disturbed when someone hinted that with so many hobbies
—physics, botany, osteology, mineralogy, geology, zoology,
anatomy, and so on, to say nothing of the plastic arts—he
must be neglecting his own proper sphere, his poetic genius.
It was as if he thought: "How do you know that poetry is not
the hobby, and that my proper sphere is not something else
entirely, namely, the Whole?" He had written a *Theory of
Colors*, in whose first draft his friend Schiller saw "many significant features of a general history of science and thought."
And in fact the historical portion of this book became, just
as Goethe intended it to be, a kind of parable of the history
of all the sciences, a novel of European thought through the
ages.

Undoubtedly he owed his tremendous prestige above all
to the scope and glory of his literary work. But there is
equally little doubt that these "hobbies" and scientific avo-
cations contributed greatly to that uncanny reputation as a
sage, that aura of power, which led to certain curious saluta-
tions in letters to him. French correspondents addressed
him as "Monseigneur," which is really the title of a prince.
An Englishman wrote: "To his Serene Highness, Prince
Goethe, in Weimar." When he passed away, the Germans
said to one another—even those who had never read a line
he had written: "Do you know what has happened? Great
Goethe has died." It sounded almost like: "Great Pan is
dead."

He often said that talent requires "a sound physical basis,"
no doubt referring to his own physique. But he also spoke of
the "feeble constitution of those who accomplish extraordinary things," and when he thus alluded to the combination of
frailty and toughness which constitutes the special vitality of

genius, he was again thinking of himself. As a matter of fact, it was usually touch and go with his health, even when there was nothing specifically wrong with him. His constitution was unstable and susceptible; from time to time severe illnesses brought him to the brink of the grave. Thus, at fifty-two he suffered an attack of erysipelas, complicated by fearful paroxysms of coughing. A lingering nervous debility followed his recuperation from this. Four years later he came down with "pulmonary fever" (perhaps pneumonia?), also accompanied by paroxysms. Continual attacks of gout and kidney stones kept him visiting the Bohemian spas early in life. During the autumn of 1823 he was in a very grave condition, physically lethargic and taking little interest in the outside world. This was the reaction to his state of ecstasy at Marienbad; it was his farewell to love; and although the subsequent illness was indefinable, it was very nearly a sickness unto death.

In short, the amity he entertained with life perpetually bordered on enmity, but he was very fond of stressing his vitality, making a great show of vim and vigor, of being a firmly rooted son of Mother Earth. He liked playing the part of the sturdy oak and boasting of his durability. And there was a good deal of robustness in his way of life. He was a heavy and fervent eater, concerned about his appetite, fond of cake and sweets, and by present-day standards virtually an alcoholic. He drank a whole bottle of wine at lunch every day, in addition to several glasses of sweet wine with his breakfast and after dinner. In those days, however, this was considered moderation. He was also inclined to joke about the infirmity of those who did not endure to the ultimate extreme. At the age of eighty-one he said: "Now consider Sömmering [a well-known German anatomist], dying at a miserable sixty-five. What a shabby lot people are, not having the courage to hold out longer than that. There's a good deal more to be said for my friend Bentham [the Eng-

lish economist and utilitarian philosopher], that radical-
minded fool. He keeps going, and he's even a few weeks
older than I am."

All very well, he spoke in jest. Nevertheless, he was setting
up a curious aristocracy of nature and vitality which in all
seriousness constituted a decisive element in his sense of his
own worth. The mockery at Bentham's "radicalism," his la-
beling it as folly, is all part of the same attitude. His interlocutor observed that if His Excellency had been born in
England he would probably also have become a radical and
entered the lists against abuses in government. Whereupon
Goethe responded with a Mephistophelean look: "What do
you think I am? Do you imagine I would have tracked down
abuses, and on top of all exposed them and made a fuss about
them? In England I would have lived by abuses. If I had been
born in England, I would have been a wealthy earl, or perhaps a bishop with an annual income of thirty thousand
pounds sterling." But he might have drawn a blank in the lot-
tery of life, his interlocutor objected; after all, there are so
many blanks. To this Goethe responded: "Not everyone, my
friend, is destined for the grand prize. Do you think I should
have committed the *bêtise* of accepting a blank?" This is arrogance, boastfulness, the rankest sense of superiority. Incidentally, it reveals that he considered his birth and life in
Germany as fundamentally a nasty trick of fate's—compared
to what would have been his lot in England. What matters
here, however, is his metaphysical certainty that in all circumstances he would have taken the grand prize, in all circumstances been well born, a child of fortune and a great
lord, a man with the world on his side—whereas it is the business of the luckless to feel indignation over the corruption of
this world.

He was fond of a phrase which logically cannot stand scru-
tiny but which fell from his lips in tones of cavalier complacency. He would speak of "innate merits." But how ab-

surd—that is like wooden iron. Merits (the word is derived
from the Latin "to earn") cannot be innate; they are acquired, won by struggle. Whatever is innate is not merited,
unless we strip the word of all its moral connotations. But
that is precisely what Goethe was doing. This phrase was a
conscious flouting of morality, of all aiming, struggling, and
striving. These are all very well, praiseworthy enough, but
not aristocratic, and at bottom he really thinks such efforts
are hopeless. "One has to *be* something," he says, "in order to
do something." In other words, merit (and blame) consists
in being, not in doing, and not, for that matter, in thinking
or saying. Existentiality, substance are what really matter—
so that a person can advocate right and it will not be right
because he is not the right person. The finest phrase in which
he expressed this faith of his in a predestined natural nobility was the following: "I hear people say: 'If only thinking
were not so hard!' The trouble is that all their thinking does
not help anyone to think; *one must be right by nature*, so that
good ideas always come before us like free children of God
and call out to us: 'Here we are!' "

Nature. Fundamentally, he had not been shaped in a paternal mold, for all that he repeated on his higher plane a good
many of his father's characteristics. He was a mother's son,
and also the favorite child, the spoiled darling, of the great
universal Mother. It was to her, Mother Nature, that he
clung, her that he trusted and thanked. That accounts for his
fortunate inclination even as a youth for Spinoza's philosophy of loving affirmation, to which he adhered to the end.
He clung to the idea of the perfection and necessity of all
that is, the conception of a world free of final causes and final
ends, in which evil as well as good is entitled to exist. "We
are fighting," he declared, "for the perfection of the work of
art in and for itself. They [the moralists] think of art's out-
ward effect, with which the true artist does not concern himself at all, no more than does Nature when she brings forth a
lion or a hummingbird." Thus, the aloofness of artistic as

well as natural creations from all purpose was his highest principle, and he regarded his innate poetic talent as "entirely nature," a gift of the all-beneficent mother who holds both good and evil alike in her embrace. In this lie the roots of his early enthusiasm for Shakespeare. Goethe's aestheticism of nature and anti-moralism was subsequently to influence Nietzsche, the immoralist, who was destined to take a further step and rapturously proclaim the primacy of evil over good, the former's overwhelming importance for the preservation and triumph of life.

In Goethe these ideas remained in calm, serene balance, remained objective and artistic convictions. But if this apotheosis of nature, this Spinozistic pantheism, was the source of his kindness, his tolerance, forbearance, and indulgence, it was also the source of his coldness, his lack of fire and idealistic élan, for which he was often reproached; of his contempt for ideas and his distaste for abstractions, which seemed to him killers of the living spirit. In one of his prose proverbs he commented: "General concepts and great conceit are always breeding dreadful calamities." This aphorism was the guiding principle of his hostility toward the French Revolution, which horrified him, troubled him as did no other public or private event in his life, and cast a pall over his poetic gifts. Yet he himself had prophetically sensed its coming, had even helped prepare the way for it with that sensational product of his youth, *Werther*—a book whose tempestuous emotionality had shaken the foundations of the old order.

His attitude toward the Revolution strikingly paralleled the attitude of Erasmus toward the Reformation, for there again a man's philosophy had paved the way for a development which the philosopher later rejected with humanistic disgust. Goethe himself coupled these two great "derangements" in the famous distich:

Franztum drängt in diesen verworrenen Tagen, wie einstmals
Luthertum es getan, ruhige Bildung zurück.

In this time of delirium Gallicism hard presses
Peaceful culture as once Lutherism had done.

Peaceful culture. It was his love of it, his constitutional
quietism and anti-vulcanism, that linked him with Erasmus.
These lines permit no doubt—if doubt should occur to anyone—of how he would have behaved in the sixteenth century,
what position he would have taken. He would have opposed
the uprising of subjects against the conservative, objective
power of the Church. And yet, like Erasmus, he too would
probably have rejected the cardinal's hat which the Pope offered to the great scholar, and which the latter refused with
graceful excuses because he was unwilling to attach himself
to the old religion, in which in his heart he no longer believed, nor to the new, which was far too uncouth for him.
Ultimately Goethe's political toryism, too, was wavering and
uncertain. In 1794, for example, a baron named Von Gagern
issued a proclamation calling upon the German intelligentsia
to use their pens in the service of the "good"—that is, the
conservative cause. In practice this meant the organization of
a new league of German princes to save the country from
"anarchy"—nowadays we would say "bolshevism." To this
appeal Duke Karl August's intimate associate replied, after
expressing polite thanks for the confidence shown him, that
he considered it "impossible for princes and writers to unite
for common action."

We find this same sort of withdrawal, this evasion of the
demands of both sides, on the part of Erasmus. It is a great
temptation to compare these celebrities of two eras and note
the similarity in their attitudes toward their times. But the
parallel tends to diminish our admiration for the charming
practitioner of irony who wrote *The Praise of Folly*. The
great humanist's all too literary subtlety, his eloquent but
thin-voiced intellectualism, ill stands comparison with the
ponderous drive, the earthy, peasant power and folk-oriented
strength of his contemporary, Luther. It suffers equally by

contrast with the cultivated nature of Goethe, who was both
an Erasmus and a Luther, who represented the union of ur-
banity and daemonic force. No combination of such persua-
sive greatness has occurred before or since in all the history
of civilization. In Goethe the folk-oriented Teutonic temper
and the European-oriented Mediterranean temper came together in a completely unforced and perfect synthesis, in a
union essentially the same as his personal fusion of genius
with rationalism, of mystery with clarity, of the cry *de pro-
fundis* with the polished phrase, of the poet with the man of
letters, of lyricism with psychology. Erasmus was a prince of
culture, but, for all the illustriousness of his figure, it lacks
entirely the wonderfully exemplary quality which was Goethe's—exemplary especially for the Germans, for he stood as
a fulfillment of ideal Germanism—and, one might add, of
ideal humanity.

Nevertheless, he inflicted a good deal of pain. Some of his
most eminent contemporaries suffered bitterly from what
Ludwig Börne called his "enormous power of obstruction,"
his indifference to politics, the weight with which he opposed, because of his very nature, the passion of his age for
the ideal of democratic nationalism. He was against freedom
of the press, against a voice for the mass of the people, against
democracy and constitutions. He was convinced that "all
good sense lies with the minority." He openly supported the
kind of cabinet minister who carries out his plans in solitary
defiance of both people and king. He had a good measure of
cordiality toward individual human beings—the sight of a
man's face, he testified, could cure him of melancholy. But
he had little or no humanitarian faith in men, in mankind, in
their susceptibility to reform or to revolutionary purifica-
tion. Men cannot be taught reason and justice, he felt. They
will eternally vacillate, and there will be no end to fighting,
no end to bloodshed. This would not have been so bad if only
he had said it with pessimistic sorrow. But, on the contrary,
he had a taste for power and its embroilments "until one man

proves his superiority over the other"—which is strongly reminiscent of Wagner's Wotan with his: "For where forces boldly fret, I candidly call for the fray." These are certainly not the sentiments of Christian charity, for all that they are Lutheran and Bismarckian as well.

Much evidence could be adduced of his quarrelsomeness, his pleasure in "pouncing down and punishing," his readiness to silence opposing opinions by the use of force and to "remove such persons from society." He admitted that he disliked "being on good terms with all and sundry," and that anger did him good. All these inclinations are, if we will, only three steps or less from brutality—and this is also true of his realism in general, of his refusal to become impassioned over ideals, of the sensuousness of his nature—so that the plundering of a farm seemed to him real and enlisted his sympathy, whereas he regarded "the ruin of the Fatherland" as an empty phrase.

The tragedy for the patriots who wished to educate Germany to the ideal of political liberty was that his incontestable greatness lent such weight of authority to his "obstructing" principles. In Germany greatness tends to a kind of hypertrophy which is in itself undemocratic. Between the great man and the common folk in Germany a gulf forms, "an emotional detachment," to use Nietzsche's favorite phrase, which does not exist to such an extent anywhere else. In other countries greatness does not produce servility on the one hand and rampant growth of absolutistic egotism on the other. Goethe in his majestic old age had a good deal of this absolutism and personal imperialism, and he exerted heavy pressure upon all the intellectuals who tried to survive alongside of him. Hence, at his death there was to be heard not only the nymphs' lament for great Pan, but a distinct "Whew" of relief.

He might regard freedom as poorly safeguarded in the hands of the servile, but for that very reason he considered himself entitled to plenty of it for himself. He took it all, took an intangible, indefinable, slippery freedom, the freedom of Proteus, which assumes all forms, insists on knowing everything, understanding everything, being everything, living inside every kind of skin. We find everything in him: romanticism and classicism, the Gothic and the Palladian, Teutonism and aristocratic rejection of popularistic patriotism, paganism and Christianity, Protestantism and Catholicism, *ancien régime* and Americanism. He was a consummation of all these movements, and there was a kind of imperial faithlessness in him, so that it would amuse him to abandon his followers, to confound the partisans of every principle by carrying it to the ultimate—and its opposite as well. He exercised a kind of universal dominion in the form of irony and serene betrayal of mutually exclusive points of view, one to the other. There was in this a profound nihilism; there was also art's—and nature's—objectivistic refusal to analyze and evaluate. There was an ambiguous impishness, an element of equivocation, negation, and all-embracing doubt which led him to make self-contradictory pronouncements. So, at any rate, his associates said. And he probably did, for how otherwise could such a woman as Charlotte von Schiller say of him: "He puts his faith in nothing." Many of his hearers speak of his disturbing indifference and disbelieving impartiality, of elements of strange malevolence and Mephistophelean negation in his attitudes. He claimed for himself a degree of ambiguity which he would permit no one else. "If I am to listen to the opinions of others," he announced, "they must be expressed positively. There is enough that is ambiguous in myself." People had to be on their toes, and talk plainly and specifically in his presence. When they did, of course, he reserved the right to think as he had thought all his life: "Good children, if only you weren't so stupid." But he would let it pass.

Let us not, however, treat the wealth and breadth of his nature, which must have seemed sinister only to limited minds, as something Mephistophelean. Rather, we may take

comfort in thinking that he was but a man with human contradictions—a great man with great, yawning contradictions.
He was fond of calling himself an "inveterate non-Christian,"
and did not trouble to conceal his proud and classical an-
tipathy to "the Cross." Certainly in his determined stress on
nature and the here-and-now there were many anti-Christian
elements which were subsequently carried to an extreme in
Nietzsche's feverish diatribes against the religion of loving-
kindness. But just as Nietzsche's baiting of Christian morality cannot but reveal an underlying asceticism, so Goethe's
notorious paganism was also predicated upon the profound-
est revolution, or rather mutation, that man's conscience and
attitude toward the cosmos has ever undergone. "There is
some divinity in all suffering." The man who spoke these
words was a Christian, for all his declarations that humility
and submission were not for him.

> *Hätt' Allah mich bestimmt zum Wurm,*
> *So hätt' er mich als Wurm erschaffen.*

> Had Allah meant me for a worm,
> As a worm he would have created me.

All very well.

> *Was bringt in Schulden?*
> *Harren und Dulden!*

> What leads to ruination?
> Patience and toleration.

So be it. And he also declared in ruthless tones that in this
life we have only the choice of being "hammer or anvil."
Nevertheless, he praised the heroic virtue of patience to the
skies, and in conversation remarked: "It seems to everyone
more praiseworthy and desirable to be the hammer rather
than the anvil, and yet what qualities it takes to endure these
everlasting, eternally recurrent blows." And what ultimately
was his attitude toward "renunciation," which more and

more became the general theme of his writing, as "freedom" did for Schiller and "redemption" for Wagner? We would think twice about calling renunciation a pagan motif. And although he was no pacifist, although he favored force, struggle, and victory, he understood precisely the nature of war. "War is in truth a disease in which the vital humors which ordinarily serve the ends of health and preservation are only employed to nourish an alien and unnatural growth."

His Christianity, as a natural component of his personality, in so far as it was not overlaid by archaizing humanism and Teutonic defiance, had a Protestant cast. His cultural background was Protestant. Indeed, a work like *The Sorrows of Werther* is inconceivable without long schooling in Pietistic introspection. His Lutheranism was deep and genuine; he felt that it corresponded to certain national and personal traits. In the part of *Faust* written while he was still in his twenties he has his hero wanting to translate the Bible, and he always paid tribute to Luther's contribution to the German language. Indeed, he assumed Luther's mantle and continued his work in the direction of further linguistic refinement. Of the Bible translation he commented: "I might have done better only in the tenderer passages."

But his Protestantism, like everything else he stood for and represented by his very being, was not altogether reliable. He was ready to admire both the aesthetic merits and the democratic, communitarian force of Catholicism. "One ought to become a Catholic," he exclaims, "in order to share in men's lives. To mingle with them on an equal plane, to live in the market place, among the people. What miserable, solitary creatures we are in our little sovereign states." And he lauds Venice as a monument to a people rather than to a ruler.

What has happened to his Teutonic aristocratism? And what has happened to his Protestant strength of character at the end of *Faust*, where he either can see no way out or, availing himself of poetic license, throws together an operatic Catholic Heaven, aromatic with incense, equipped with *mater gloriosa*, penitents, blessed boys, choirs of angels, *pater profundus* and *pater seraphicus*? Nor was that the limit, for how far he goes in his novel *The Elective Affinities*, where he sponsors Catholicism to the extent of setting up a saint in the midst of a Protestant environment, and having Lutheran country folk believing in miracles and thronging to the church to venerate the saint's body. And yet the nature fatalism of this masterpiece is not Christian at all—the more so since this fatalism continues to operate in the hereafter, in which no character in the book really believes. The concluding words about the compulsive lovers who awake amiably together from the sleep of death is no more than a conciliatory flourish.

His was a mind that could not be pinned down to anything, could not be assigned any one view. Classify him where you will in the realm of thought and life; you will be right, and will at once reconsider and discover that he is also the opposite. This principle extends to his ethics, to his attitude toward time, for example. In part he generously allowed himself all the time in the world, delayed, postponed, took it easy, passively and vegetatively left things to take their course. And then again he practiced a veritable worship of time, carefully guarding, holding, cultivating, turning to profit the gift of time according to the motto:

> *Mein Erbteil wie herrlich, weit und breit!*
> *Die Zeit ist mein Besitz, mein Acker die Zeit.*

> How lordly my heritage, what a noble expanse!
> For time my estate is, time my broad lands.

And according to that French motto: *Le temps est le seul dont l'avarice soit louable*—Time is the one thing of which we should be miserly.

The same dividedness extends into the artistic realm,

where he purports to be the great objectivist, the ironic Apollonian, and where he was simultaneously lyricist and autobiographer *par excellence* who always derived everything from himself, always gave only of himself, and had his greatest influence in France precisely because of this romantic subjectivism. Confession he certainly went in for, in a curiously radical and penitential manner. For how does he make these confidences? By depicting scoundrels and weaklings: Werther the suicide, Clavigo the traitor, Tasso the hysteric; spineless Eduard, or the frankly silly Fernando in *Stella*. We wonder how, with such a gallery of characters, he dares to make fun of "hospital poetry" and demand instead what he calls "Tyrtaean"—that is, inspiring—verse. What he gives us is a hospital, too, filled with psychology, confessions, revelations of all too human weaknesses. Even Wilhelm Meister and Faust leave a good deal to be desired as models of manhood and stalwart character—if this should be what we are looking for.

But if his varied creations are not so exceedingly masculine (Schiller's are far more so), they are by way of compensation honestly, candidly human, human in the extreme. Moreover—or therefore—they bear in every line and every turn of phrase the personal mark of a charm whose like cannot easily be found in all the broad realms of literature. As evidence of this I like to adduce his *Egmont*, a play by no means beyond criticism on dramaturgical and artistic grounds. Yet its unconcern with theatrical principles accords remarkably with the character of the hero, that gallantly popularistic and sinfully careless grand seigneur, that daemonically frivolous favorite of the gods and of men, whose figure the poet makes the center of all interest. To my mind, Egmont represents the quintessence of that special Goethean charm—among other things in his strikingly dispassionate, tenderly condescending, and somewhat narcissistic relationship with Klärchen, the little girl of the people who is a true sister of Faust's Gretchen. What narcissism in his presenting himself to her in his Spanish court costume with the Order of the Golden Fleece, so that he may enjoy her childish ah's and oh's. What self-mirroring eroticism this is, which is so intrigued by the idea of a sweet and simple young thing receiving a visitant from a brilliant, alien world of high thought and love who finds it all too easy to displace her honest middle-class adorer and suitor. The penitent guilt feeling of the seducer, who has no thought of marriage, who is forever amorous and will not tie himself down, is part of the picture.

Goethe's love life is a strange chapter. The list of his love affairs has become a requirement of education; in respectable German society one has to be able to rattle off the ladies like the loves of Zeus. Those Friederikes, Lottes, Minnas, and Mariannes have become statues installed in niches in the cathedral of humanity; and perhaps this makes amends to them for their disappointments. For the fickle genius who for short whiles lay at their feet was never prepared to take the consequences, to bear the restriction upon his life and liberty that these charming adventures might have involved. Perhaps the fame of the ladies is compensation to them for his recurrent flights, for the aimlessness of his wooing, the faithlessness of his sincerity, and the fact that his loving was a means to an end, a means to further his work. Where work and life are one, as was the case with him, those who know only how to take life seriously are left with all the sorrows in their laps. But he always reproved them for taking life seriously. "Werther must—must be!" he wrote to Lotte Buff and her fiancé. "You two do not feel *him*, you feel only *me* and *yourselves*. . . . If only you could feel the thousandth part of what Werther means to a thousand hearts, you would not reckon the cost to you." All his women bore the cost, whether they liked it or not.

From the very beginning he wrote, wrote in anacreontic, French, sportive, talented, and conventional styles. But he became a true poet in Strassburg, under Herder's influence and

through the tremendous liberating power of contact with
Homer, with Macpherson-Ossian, with Shakespeare (for
whom all his life he felt unlimited admiration and whom he
rated high above himself), with the Bible as literature, and,
above all, with folk songs, in whose dewy freshness, wholesome rhythms, simple language, and emotional force his own
lyrics were steeped.

By virtue of his broad knowledge, his insight, and a critic's feeling for essentials, Herder should have been leader of
the revolutionary literary sentiments which, in the Germany
of around 1770, were only waiting to be rallied. But he
lacked what his pupil Goethe, five years his junior, possessed: fascination, grace, the compelling mystery of personality. In his immaturity Goethe had been only too ready to
regard himself as a mere planet orbiting around the mighty
star which Herder already was. As it turned out, Goethe was
the sun around which the new intellectual life of Germany
was destined to revolve. I imagine that Herder sensed this
quite soon, and that the other's precedence was a bitter pill to
swallow. In his attitude toward the patiently respectful
younger man it is hard to distinguish the pedagogical impulse
from rancor, even from a profound love-hatred. He made
Goethe the butt of everlasting mockery and ridicule, descended even to sneering at his name, which, he pointed out,
might equally well be derived from *Kot* (ordure) as from
Gothe (Goth) or *Gott* (god). He carped at Goethe's lack of
discrimination and good taste, his affectations, and so on. In
his old age he finally went too far with his now great patron.
He made an imprudent joke about Goethe's actually rather
boring revolutionary drama *The Natural Daughter*. "I prefer your natural son," he remarked. That finished off their
old friendship.

Nowadays we can scarcely imagine the excitement, the
surge of intellectual rejoicing, inspired in that springtide of
genius, that period of storm and stress, by such a poem as
Willkommen und Abschied (*Welcome and Farewell*):

Mir schlug das Herz, geschwind zu Pferde!
Und fort! wild, wie ein Held zur Schlacht.
Der Abend wiegte schon die Erde
Und an den Bergen hing die Nacht;
Schon stund im Nebelkleid die Eiche
Ein aufgetürmter Riese da,
Wo Finsternis aus dem Gesträuche
Mit hundert schwarzen Augen sah.

> My heart beat high! To horse, to horse!
> Away! like a warrior to the fray.
> Already the sun had run his course
> And night upon the mountain lay.
> All robed in mist the oak tree stood,
> A monster, towering and weird,
> While darkness from the glowering wood
> With hundred eyes of blackness peered.

How new, how bold, how wonderfully free, melodious, and picturesque that was! The gusts of these rhythms made the powder fly from rationalistic wigs. So was it also with his "dramatic history" of *Götz von Berlichingen*, that fling at Shakespearean drama, that series of tableaux of the German past so bursting with vitality. Frederick the Great dismissed it as formless rot. But in German lands it aroused enthusiasm by its hearty affront to the stuffy rules of poetry, aroused also that "national pleasure" which Goethe so gracefully depicts in his autobiography, *Poetry and Truth*. And then the first scenes of *Faust*, fresh from his pen—it is easy to believe that his friends clapped their hands in wonder at the way "the fellow was visibly growing."

From the beginning *The Sorrows of Werther* outran the confines of his friends, his coterie, his school, and his nation. The world seized upon it; it seized upon the world. The distressing, unsettling sentimentality of this epistolary novel, which horrified and disgusted the moralists in spite of its large admixture of sincerity, love for nature, and youthful metaphysical flights, was met with an acclaim which exceeded all bounds. It summoned up an intoxication, a fever, an ecstasy that raced over the inhabited earth. Its effect was that of a spark in a powder keg: the sudden expansion of dangerously confined forces. We must suppose that the little book encountered a general state of readiness. It was as though the public of all countries, obscurely and unwittingly, had been waiting for this very work from the pen of an unimportant young citizen of a German imperial city. The work released at one revolutionary stroke the chained desires of a whole civilization. It was a bolt that hit its target squarely. Napoleon, the iron man, the child of Nemesis, carried the French translation on his Egyptian campaign. He said that he had read it seven times.

As an author Goethe never again had such a wild triumph. His work, that tremendous track left by his life, was never again greeted by such mass enthusiasm. The German public remained completely cool to the classicism he began to practice in *Iphigenia* and *Tasso*. The public did not feel the enchanting, piquant contrast between classical form and the poetic intimacy and daring content he poured into that form. True, *Wilhelm Meister* was a great success in its time, both in circulation and in its effect upon its readers—so much so that a member of the Romantic movement, which then represented the summit of German culture, could declare: "The French Revolution, Fichte's theory of science, and *Wilhelm Meister* are the three great events of the age." But, for all the numerous literary descendants of this classical German *Bildungsroman* or novel of spiritual and psychological growth—a line which extends through Stifter and Keller to *The Magic Mountain*—*Meister* never won anything like the instantaneous raging success of *Werther*. This was still more true of *The Elective Affinities*, that novel of the mystic dominance of nature over human psychology. The characters are true to life and individually convincing, but they are also symbols, chess pieces of a sixty-year-old writer, evenly grouped and

moved about in a lofty intellectual game. Nevertheless, this
book provoked one of the neatest characterizations of Goethe's prose when, after reading the novel, his friend Zelter,
the composer, wrote to him from Berlin: "There are certain
symphonies of Haydn which by their easy, unchecked flow
stir my blood pleasurably. . . . That is always my sensation when I read your novels, and particularly so now as I
read your *Elective Affinities*. You never falter in your sportive, mysterious play with the things of the world and the
characters whom you set up and direct, for all the extraneous
elements which find or thrust their way into the work. Your
feat is assisted by a style which resembles that transparent
element whose nimble denizens swim to and fro like bright
flashes or dark shadows, without ever going astray or losing
their way. Such prose is enough to drive one to verse, and
the devil knows that I personally could not write a single
line like one of yours." It was reserved to a musician to properly appreciate the precision and agility of Goethe's prose, its
rhythmic charm which without ever departing from rationality weaves a spell over the reader, its crystal-clear fusion of
Eros and Logos.

The first edition of the *Westöstlicher Diwan*, which contained priceless pearls of Goethe's late lyrics, had no sale at
all and ended up as wastepaper. Summoning all his forces in a
last effort which we find truly moving, the old man rounded
off the second part of *Faust* (he did not complete it, for it
could not be completed) and sealed it up. During his lifetime,
he said, he was unwilling to communicate "these very earnest
jests" even to his many "gratefully acknowledged" friends
throughout Europe, still less to the public. For, he declared,
"the times are really so absurdly confused that I believe my
grave and prolonged labors upon this strange structure would
be poorly rewarded, and the work itself driven to the beach
to lie in ruins like a wreck, soon to be drifted over by the
sand-dunes of the hours." Clearly, the old man expresses himself still in the forceful imagery of his youth, though there is

another accent here, the words ringing with the pathos and dignity of advanced age, of fading creativity on the point of retiring from this temporal world.

It happened as he had thought. His labors upon that "strange structure," labors which lasted all his life, were never well rewarded. True, the first part of *Faust*, written in his youth, enjoyed a kind of popularity quotationwise, at least among the cultivated German middle class. The second part has been honored, admired, plowed thoroughly by scholars, but it has been far less loved. It has always been regarded as a prodigy of allegorical mystification, all very well as a "national property" but queer and unpalatable. I have never understood this—or at any rate have for a very long time been unable to understand it. Certainly this "incommensurable" work (but what is really interesting aside from the incommensurable?) is open to criticism on moral and even artistic grounds. Monstrous it certainly is, and yet this product of slow time is not too vast to be grasped, not too deep to be penetrated. Half cosmic poem, half elaborate revue, comprehending three thousand years of history from the fall of Troy to the siege of Missolonghi, a glorious spectacle of all the leaping founts of language, it is throughout so excellent, so brilliant, so felicitous in its verbal expression and so abounding in wisdom and wit, so artistically joyous, gay and light in its profundities and its greatness—in the humorous treatment of mythology, for example (the Pharsalian Fields and the Upper Peneios, the Mystery of Helen)—that every contact with it delights, amazes, animates, inspires to artistic production. For, more than reverence, this eternally curious structure deserves love. Indeed, it is a tremendous temptation to write a wholly fresh, wholly unscholarly and direct commentary on *Faust* which might reassure the timid reader who superstitiously quails before a poem which is charming even where it seems to be at its wits' end.

Incidentally, portions of the second part of *Faust* were published during Goethe's lifetime. The Helen episode was

brought out, and Goethe lived to read solemn reviews of it
in many great foreign periodicals, French, Scottish, and Russian. As things stood, everything he wrote had long been regarded by authoritative critics as world literature. He himself had coined the word *Weltliteratur*, by which he meant
partly a fact and partly a challenge. The term suited his personal tendency to universalism, which grew constantly
stronger in his old age. That is normal enough in a writer
whose career began with so international a success as *Werther*. But he intended the term also as an instructive reprimand to his Germans. "Instead of keeping himself to himself," he told them, "the German must take the world into
himself in order to influence the world. . . . For that reason
I like to look into what other nations have to offer and would
advise everyone to do likewise. National literature is of no
great importance nowadays; the era of world literature is
dawning, and everyone must do his part to hasten its arrival."

Certainly he did take the world into himself, and influence
the world. What England, Italy, France, Spain, the Far East,
and America gave to him, and what his work contributed to
the intellectual life of those and other lands—this process of
systole and diastole has recently been described by the literary critic Fritz Strich, of Bern, in his admirable study *Goethe
und die Weltliteratur* (*Goethe and World Literature*). It is a
truly comprehensive view, valuable precisely because it pre-
sents Goethe's Europeanism in both the subjective and objective aspects, in terms of what the great man received as
well as what he gave.

It is quite clear that the concept of "world literature" was
a product of both giving and receiving, that it was based
on more than Goethe's awareness of the sources of his own
culture and of his personal debt to the great art of other
lands; the idea also sprang from observation of the effect of
his own work. Moreover, it is a term which quite belongs in
the vocabulary of greatness—that greatness into which the
boy from Frankfurt was destined to grow. For he did grow

into greatness, although the septuagenarian confessed that he
had had "a hard time learning" its ways, learning to influence
his country and his age. In an aphorism written in old age
he says:

Wer nicht von dreitausend Jahren
Sich weiß Rechenschaft zu geben,
Bleib' im Dunkel unerfahren,
Mag von Tag zu Tage leben.

> If the past three thousand years
> Do not lie in your survey,
> For you the darkness never clears;
> You must live from day to day.

Faust was the amazing product of this inner spaciousness,
this encyclopedic command of the world. Commenting on
the Helen episode in particular and on the whole of *Faust* in
general, Emerson said: "The remarkable thing about it is the
tremendous intelligence. The intellect of this man is such a
powerful solvent that past ages and the present, their reli-
gions, politics, and modes of thought resolve themselves into
their elements and ideas." But this "tremendous intelligence,"
this limitless, organizing, and alchemistic intelligence, by no
means serves solely to make a synopsis of past and present.
It is equally bold in its sense of the future, in foreseeing and
anticipating things to come, the things that are "dawning,"
of which "world literature" is only a symbol, a shorthand
abbreviation. He sometimes described it as "free trade in
ideas and emotions," a truly Goethean transference of liberal
economic principles to the life of the intellect.

Such views are of the nineteenth century, the century of
economics and technology. We must not forget that this son
of the eighteenth century lived for the span of a whole generation into the nineteenth, and that he "grasped" the future
far beyond the limits of his own life, beyond the limits of the
century itself, and prophesied the post-bourgeois age. There
is a curious poignancy to this: that the last years of his life

were thus given to this death-defying quest, this urgent
reaching out beyond his own death to sense the things that
were "dawning," both in the moral realm and in practical
life and technology. Since these things were coming, he believed, it was incumbent upon everyone to speed them on
their way, even at the cost of long-cherished but outmoded
ideas. Certainly there is a great deal of "renunciation" in
Wilhelm Meisters Wanderjahre, written in his old age—the
voluntary abandonment, for example, of individualism in favor of more humane and social-minded principles which
properly belong to our own times. The book flashes with
lightning bolts of ideas that far transcend the bourgeois conception of man, far transcend the classical and middle-class
view of culture which Goethe himself had primarily helped
to build. The ideal of personal many-sidedness is cast aside;
Goethe suddenly proclaims a dawning age of specialization.
He recognizes the inadequacy of the individual, a concept so
prevalent today. Only collectively can men complete the
work of humanity, he declares. The individual serves a
function; the question is: What can be done for culture by
and through him? The concept of community, of a social
bond, emerges. The Jesuitically strict discipline of society
depicted in the *Pedagogical Province*—for all the honor
paid there to the Muses—is a far cry from the "liberal" bourgeois ideal.

What an old age! Despite his dignity, he had nothing of
the desiccated or ossified about himself. To the end he remained sensitive, curious, full of life, eager to promote new
things. At table with this ceremonious eighteenth-century
grand seigneur there was more talk about steamships and
early experiments with a flying machine, about utopian
technological problems and projects, than about literature
and poetry. And shall we wonder at this in the poet who
makes Faust feel his greatest triumph in the realization of a
utilitarian dream, the draining of a swamp? The old man
never tired of exploring the possibilities of connecting the

Gulf of Mexico with the Pacific Ocean; never tired of describing the incalculable gains such a project would bring to the whole of the civilized and the still uncivilized world. He recommended that the United States of America take the business in hand, and conjured up fantasies of flourishing ports gradually growing along this Pacific Coast, where nature had so happily prepared the way by creating ample harbors. He could scarcely wait for the accomplishment of these projects, these and the linking of the Danube and the Rhine—although this last would be a far more formidable task than anyone imagined. He also looked forward to a third, immense enterprise—a Suez canal, for the English. "To see all these things," he exclaimed, "it would probably be worth while to stick it out for another fifty years or so on this earth."

Thus, his excitement over the future was all-embracing; it took in the entire world. And there was an element of magnificent soberness in this enthusiasm for global, technological, rational matters. It was as if he felt the necessity for restoring sobriety to a world grown ill on musty sentimentalities that poisoned the bloodstream of life.

> *Amerika, du hast es besser*
> *Als unser Kontinent, der alte*
> *Hast keine verfallenen Schlösser*
> *Und keine Basalte.*

> America, you're better off than
> Our continent so antiquary.
> You have no castles falling down,
> No marble statuary.

Ruined citadels and all too venerable petrifications are the "dead rot" of which he speaks elsewhere, and which man must escape in order to love living things. They are the symbols of a burden of sentiment which the poet nearly equates with the "killing stupidity" he fought in his youth, when he threw in his lot with clear intelligence. "The human rabble," he had written in *Wilhelm Meister*, "is afraid of nothing so much as intelligence; if they understood what is truly fearful, they would fear stupidity. But intelligence generates discomfort, and therefore must be eliminated immediately; stupidity is only ruinous, and it is not hard to wait for ruin to come."

Awaiting the coming ruin without the courage to call in intelligence—has not this tendency and this danger to humanity reached its peak today? Goethe knew the power of stupidity; he saw it growing, and this essentially was what he pitted his greatness against, far more than he pitted it against revolution, constitutionality, freedom of the press, or democracy. It is said that his last words before he passed into his final sleep were: "Let in more light." At least these are his proverbial last words. But his true last words, the words he undeniably said from first to last, were directed against death and in support of life:

"In the end, the only way to move is forward!"

Translated by Richard and Clara Winston

NIETZSCHE'S PHILOSOPHY IN THE LIGHT
OF RECENT HISTORY

WHEN at the beginning of the year 1889 word spread of Nietzsche's mental breakdown, there must already have been a good many persons here and there in Europe who knew the stature of the man and could have mourned like Ophelia: "O, what a noble mind is here o'erthrown."

Phrase after phrase in the lines which follow, lines which deplore the tragedy that such a majestic intellect should be "blasted with ecstasy" and sound now like jangled bells, might well apply to Nietzsche—most notably, perhaps, the expression: "The observ'd of all observers." Nowadays we might make use of the word "fascinating." And, truly, we may search the history of literature and philosophy in vain for a more fascinating figure than that of the hermit of Sils Maria. But it is a fascination closely akin to that which through the centuries has emanated from Shakespeare's melancholy Dane.

Nietzsche, the philosopher and writer, "the mould of form," as Ophelia would call him, was a phenomenon of vast cultural scope and complexity, a veritable résumé of the European spirit. He had absorbed many elements of the past, and in more or less consciously emulating them called them again to mind, restored them in mythic fashion to contemporary significance. I do not doubt that this great lover of masquerade was well aware of the Hamlet role he played in the tragic spectacle which was his life—I might almost say, in the tragedy he staged. I myself, the deeply moved, fascinated "observer" and reader of the following generation, was struck almost from the start by the resemblance to Hamlet. The emotion which came to me was one the youthful mind in particular finds new, stirring, and profound: a combination of reverence and pity. It is an emotion which I have never ceased to feel toward Nietzsche. Its central factor is tragic pity for an overburdened soul, a soul upon whom too many charges have been laid—one only called to knowledge, but not really born for it and, like Hamlet, shattered by it; a delicate, fine, warmhearted soul in need of love, formed for noble friendships and not at all made for solitude. And upon this soul deepest, coldest solitude, the solitude of the criminal, was imposed. Here was a mind by origin profoundly respectful, shaped to revere pious traditions; and just such a mind fate chose to drag by the hair, as it were, into a posture of wild and drunken truculence, of rebellion against all reverence. This mind was compelled to violate its own nature, to become the mouthpiece and advocate of blatant brute force, of the callous conscience, of Evil itself.

We must look at the origins of this mind, take note of the influences which shaped Nietzsche's personality—influences which he considered in no wise incongruous—in order to grasp the fantastical nature of his development, its complete unpredictability. Born in rural Central Germany in 1844, four years before the German middle class attempted a revolution, Nietzsche was descended, on both the paternal and maternal sides, from a line of respected clergymen. Ironically enough, his grandfather had written a tract on *The Everlasting Permanence of Christianity—for Reassurance in the Present Ferment.* His father was in some degree a courtier, having acted as tutor of the Prussian princesses, and owed his pastorate to the favor of Frederick William IV. Thus, a feeling for aristocratic forms, strict morals, high probity, and punctilious orderliness prevailed in the Nietzsche household. After his father's early death the boy lived in Naumburg, a city of officials noted for their observance of religious forms and their royalist sentiments. He is described as "fearfully well-behaved," a notorious model boy, grave of demeanor and exceedingly pious, so that he early earned the nickname of "the little pastor." Thus, there is the well-known anecdote of his walking home from school in a sudden downpour at a dignified and measured pace—because the school rules called for decorous conduct in the streets. He completed his secondary schooling brilliantly in the famous convent school of Schulpforta. Although his inclinations drew him to theology and music, he decided to specialize in classical philology, and pursued this study at the University of Leipzig under a strict systematician named Ritschl. Again he acquitted himself brilliantly and, after his spell of military service in the artillery, was called to teach at the University of Basel, that grave, pious, patrician-ruled city.

In all this we can picture a man whose high intellectual endowments and unexceptionable propriety would seem to guarantee a respectable career on a distinguished plane. And instead, starting from such solid footing, how he was driven forward into pathless wastes! Like the Alpinist who climbs too high among the glacial peaks until he reaches the point of no return where he can move neither forward nor backward, he overreached himself. It smacks of philistinism to say that Nietzsche aimed too high, or to dub as "high-flown" the man who was undoubtedly the greatest philosopher of the close of the nineteenth century, as well as one of the most intrepid heroes who ever ventured into the realm of thought. But Jakob Burckhardt, to whom Nietzsche looked up as to a father, was no philistine; and yet he early observed in his younger friend the tendency, and even the determination, to overreach himself, to climb to the fatal height where advance and retreat alike become impossible. And Burckhardt prudently saw to it that their ways parted; he dropped Nietzsche with an aplomb that reminds one of Goethe's instinct for sparing himself such unfortunate involvements.

But what was it that drove Nietzsche upward into the pathless wastes, lashed him on to the tortuous climb, and brought him to a martyr's death on the cross of thought? It was his destiny—and his destiny was his genius. But there is another name for this genius: disease. The word is to be taken not in the vague and general sense in which it is so often used in conjunction with the idea of genius, but in so specific and clinical a sense that we once again court the suspicion of vulgarity and the charge that we would devaluate the creative achievements of a thinker, psychologist, and master of language who revolutionized the whole atmosphere of his era. Let us clear away this misunderstanding. It has often been said, and I now say it again: Disease is a mere category which derives its meaning from what it is coupled with, whom it belongs to. What matters is *who* is sick: an ordinary blockhead, in whom the disease has no intellectual or cultural aspects—or a Nietzsche, a Dostoevsky. Medical pathology is one side of the truth—its naturalistic side, so to speak. The lover of the whole truth, who is prepared to pay homage to truth without reservations, will not be bound by intellectual prudery, will not repudiate any point of view which offers an additional insight. Dr. Paul Julius Möbius has been severely censured for having written a book in which he described Nietzsche's development as a case history in progressive syphilis. I have never been able to share this censure. In his own fashion the good doctor has told the incontestable truth.

In 1865 the twenty-one-year-old Nietzsche told Paul Deussen, his fellow student and later a famous Sanskrit scholar, a curious story. The young man had gone on an outing to Cologne by himself, and there engaged a guide to show him the sights of the city. They went about all afternoon, until at last, toward evening, Nietzsche asked to be taken to a good restaurant. But the man, whom I have always envisioned as a kind of devil's emissary, took him to a brothel. The boy, pure as a maiden, the soul of scholarship, intellectuality, innocent timidity, found himself suddenly surrounded by, as he put it, half a dozen apparitions in gauze and spangles who looked expectantly at him. The young musician, philologian, and admirer of Schopenhauer made his way between them and instinctively went up to a piano which he had descried at the back of this fiendish parlor. He regarded it (these are his own words) as "the only being with a soul in this company." He struck a few chords. The action broke the spell, routed his numbness, and he was able to escape, to rush out into the street.

Next day he related this experience to his friend—no doubt having a hearty laugh over it. He was unconscious of the impression the incident had made upon him. But it had been nothing more nor less than what psychologists call a "trauma," a shock whose steadily accumulating aftereffects —from which his imagination never recovered—testify to the saint's receptivity to sin. In the fourth part of *Zarathustra*, written twenty years later, there is to be found in the chapter "Among the Daughters of the Desert" an orientalized poem whose grotesquely jesting tone betrays, with painful tastelessness, the pangs of mortified sensuality. The inhibitions are gone, but the embarrassment remains. In this poem concerning "those dearest wenches and girl-cats Dudu and Suleika" —an erotic fantasy whose waggishness makes one distinctly uncomfortable—the "flittery, fluttery petticoats" of the professional ladies of Cologne reappear once again. The "apparitions in gauze and spangles" obviously served as models for the delightful daughters of the desert. And from these first he had not far to go—only four years, in fact—to the clinic in Basel where the patient stated for the medical record that he had been specifically infected twice in previous years. The medical history preserved at Jena gives the year 1866 for the first of these misadventures. In other words, one year after he had fled from the house in Cologne he returned —without diabolic guidance, this time—to some similar place and contracted the disease (some say deliberately, as self-punishment) which was to destroy his life but also to intensify it enormously. Indeed, that disease in Nietzsche was to exert stimulating effects in part beneficial, in part deadly, upon an entire era.

What spurred him to leave his academic post at Basel after a few years was a compound of failing health and the urge toward freedom. At bottom these are the same. This young admirer of Wagner and Schopenhauer had early proclaimed art and philosophy as the true guides to life—as against history, of which his own specialty, philology, is a branch. He turned away from philology, obtained a pension on grounds of illness, and henceforth lived without ties, an unassuming gentleman lodger, at international resorts in Italy, the South of France, the Swiss mountains. Subsisting thus modestly, he wrote his stylistically dazzling books—works sparkling with audacious insults to his age, venturing into more and more radical psychology, radiating a more and more glaring white light. In a letter he called himself "a man who wishes nothing more than daily to lose some reassuring belief, who seeks and finds his happiness in this daily greater liberation of the mind." He adds: "It may be that I want to be even more of a freethinker than I can be." This confession was made very early, in 1876, and it constitutes an anticipation of his fate, of his going to smash. It was the premonition of a man who will be driven to saddle himself with insights crueler than his temperament can bear, and who will offer the world the heartbreaking spectacle of self-crucifixion.

He might very well have written beneath his work, as did that painter: "*In doloribus pinxi.*" In more than one sense, in a physical as well as spiritual sense, he would have been stating only the blunt truth. In 1880 he admitted to a physician, Dr. Eiser: "My existence is a frightful burden; I would long ago have cast it aside if it were not that in this very state of suffering and of almost absolute renunciation I am able to make the most instructive tests and experiments in the ethical and spiritual realms. . . . Constant pain, a sensation akin to seasickness for several hours a day, semi-paralysis in which speech is difficult for me, by way of change furious convulsions (in the throes of the last I vomited for three days and nights; I thirsted for death). . . . If only I could describe to you the continuousness of it, the constant pain and pressure in the head and on the eyes, and that numbed sensation throughout my body, from the head to the tips of my toes! . . ." His apparently complete ignorance—and that of his doctors also!—as to the nature and cause of these sufferings is difficult to understand. In the course of time he became certain that the disease had its source in the brain, and he thought it was of hereditary origin. His father, he believed, had died of "softening of the brain"—which was certainly not the case. Pastor Nietzsche died by sheer accident, of an injury to the brain incurred from a fall. This total ignorance, or this dissimulation of knowledge, of the origin of his disease can be explained only by the fact that it was coupled and interlinked with his genius, that his genius developed along with the disease, and that to an inspired psychologist everything is grist to the mills of his merciless insight—except his own genius.

This genius of his became rather the object of his wonderstruck admiration, of exuberant self-assertiveness, crass *hubris*. With complete naïveté Nietzsche glorified the blissful obverse of his disease, those euphoric compensations and overcompensations which are part of the clinical picture. He did this most magnificently in the almost entirely uninhibited late work *Ecce homo*, especially in the passage hailing the wonderfully elevated physical and intellectual state in which he had written his Zarathustra poem in so incredibly short a time. The page is a stylistic masterpiece, a veritable linguistic tour de force, comparable only to the marvelous analysis of the prelude to the *Meistersinger* in *Beyond Good and Evil* and to the dionysiac description of the cosmos at the end of *The Will to Power*. "Has anyone," he asks in *Ecce homo*, "at the end of the nineteenth century a conception of what the poets of *strong* ages called inspiration? If not, I will describe it." And now there begins a description of illuminations, ecstasies, elations, exaltations, feelings of divine power, which he takes as something atavistic, daemonically derivative from other, "stronger," states when man stood closer to the gods, states of being utterly exceptional, lifted far above the physical potentialities of our feeble, rational epoch. What he is "in truth" describing—but what is truth, the experience or its medical interpretation?—is a dangerous condition of overstimulation which ironically precedes tertiary-luetic collapse.

Everyone will grant that Nietzsche's paeans to his own work are delirious excesses of egotism. It is certainly evidence of vanishing rationality when he calls *Zarathustra* an act compared to which all the rest of human achievements appear poor and petty; when he asserts that a Goethe, a Shakespeare, or a Dante would not for a moment be able to breathe at the altitude attained by this book; or that the talents of all great minds taken together would be incapable of producing even one of his Zarathustra's orations. Of course it must be most gratifying to write down such sentiments, but it really is impermissible. However, it may be that I am only exposing my own inadequacy when I go further and state that in general Nietzsche's relationship to his *Zarathustra* seems to me one of blind overestimation. The book has become, thanks to its Biblical pose, the most "popular" of his works, but it is far from his best. Nietzsche was, above all, a great critic and philosopher of culture, a European prose-writer and essayist of the very first rank—in this sense, too, he was a disciple of Schopenhauer. His genius reached its height at the time he wrote *Beyond Good and Evil* and *The Genealogy of Morals*. A creative writer may be something less than such a critic; but, however that may be, Nietzsche did not have the faculty to be that something less. Or if he did, it was only in isolated moments of lyricism, not through an extended work of creative originality. This faceless and bodiless monstrosity, this drum major Zarathustra with laughter's crown of roses upon his disfigured head, his "Become hard!" and his dancer's legs, is not a character; he is rhetoric, wild verbiage and puns, a tormented voice and dubious prophecy, a phantom of pitiable grandezza, often touching and usually embarrassing—an abortion bordering on the verge of the ludicrous.

In saying this I recall the desperate cruelty with which Nietzsche spoke of all that he himself venerated: of Wagner, music in general, morality, Christianity—I almost said, of Germanism as well. Yet even in the midst of his most ferocious critical assaults upon these values and forces which within himself he always cherished, he obviously never felt that he was harming them. Rather, it would seem, he regarded the most rabid of the insults he hurled at them as a form of homage. He said such things about Wagner that we do not believe our eyes when in *Ecce homo* he suddenly refers to the *holy* hour when Richard Wagner died in Venice. How, we may ask, has this hour of his death become sanctified if Wagner were the meretricious sham, the corrupt corrupter, that Nietzsche branded him a hundred times over? . . . Or, again, Nietzsche apologized to his friend Peter Gast, the musician, for constantly quarreling with Christianity; after all, he said, it represented the finest ideal he had ever known, and he himself was the descendant of whole generations of Christian clergymen. He believed, he went on, that he had "never been, in his heart, insulting to Christianity." True enough, though in an overwrought moment he had called it "the one immortal blot of shame upon the escutcheon of humanity." At the same time he had ridiculed the thesis that the Teuton was somehow predestined to adopt Christianity. What had that bellicose and rapacious sluggard, that sensually cold lover of the hunt and guzzler of beer, who had never himself got any further than a rough-and-tumble Red Indian religion and who only a thousand years ago had slaughtered human beings upon stone altars—what had he to do with the most sublime moral subtlety, sharpened by rabbinical analysis? What had he to do with the Oriental refinement of Christianity? His true opinion is transparent and amusing. This "Antichrist" gave the most Christian of all titles to his autobiography: *Ecce homo*. And last scraps of paper he wrote in his madness were signed: "The Crucified One."

We may say that Nietzsche's relationship to the preferred objects of his criticism was simply one of passion—a passion without specific sign, for it was constantly shifting between positive and negative. A little while before the end of his mental life, he wrote a page on *Tristan* which quivered with enthusiasm. On the other hand, even during the days when he apparently was an out-and-out Wagner disciple, before he wrote the public tribute contained in *Richard Wagner in Bayreuth*, he had privately made slurring remarks on *Lohengrin* to friends in Basel. These remarks betrayed so cold a perspicacity that they certainly anticipated his *The Case of Wagner* of more than fifteen years later. Say what you will, there was no break in Nietzsche's relationship to Wagner. The world loves to find sharp cleavages in the life and work of great men. Such a cleavage has been found in Tolstoy, though all his doctrinaire teachings, all his later views, can be seen psychologically foreshadowed in his early work. Another has been found in Wagner himself, whose development was guided by a similar unswerving continuity and logic. The case of Nietzsche is no different. Much as his largely aphoristic work glitters in a thousand colored facets, many as are the surface contradictions that can be demonstrated in his books—he was from the start a coherent whole, remained always the same. In the writings of the youthful professor—the *Thoughts Out of Season*, *The Birth of Tragedy*, and the 1873 treatise *The Philosopher*—are to be found more than the seeds of his later dogmas, the tidings he was to hurl down from his mountaintop. More than seeds because these dogmas—which in his opinion were *glad* tidings—were already contained in perfect and finished form in those works. What changed was solely the accentuation, the pitch, the gestures. These grew steadily more frantic, shriller, more grotesque and terrible. What changed was the style, which continued to be musical, but gradually degenerated from the rather old-fashioned scholarly discipline and restraint of the humanistic German tradition into an unhealthy sophisticated and feverishly gay super-journalism, which in the end he adorned with the cap and bells of a cosmic jester.

Still, we cannot sufficiently stress the complete unity and coherence of Nietzsche's life work. He remained Schopenhauer's disciple long after he had rejected his master; and all his life he was really doing no more than vary, expand, hammer away at one ubiquitous idea. At first he developed it sanely and soundly, employing it for a well-merited critique of his times. With the passing years the idea fell victim to a maenadic savagery, so that we may call Nietzsche's biography the history of the decay of this idea.

What is this idea? It must be broken up into its ingredients, and its contending elements within his personality analyzed, if we are to understand it. Those elements, named as they come to mind, are: life, culture, consciousness or cognition, art, nobleness, morality, instinct. The dominant notion in this whole complex is that of culture, which is equated almost with life itself. Culture for Nietzsche is the aristocracy of life; and linked with it, as its sources and prerequisites, are art and instinct, whereas the mortal enemies and destroyers of culture and life are consciousness and cognition, science, and finally morality. Morality, as the guardian of truth, attacks the very core of life, since life is essentially based upon appearance, art, deception, perspective, and illusion. Error, Nietzsche avers, is the parent of all vitality.

Nietzsche inherited from Schopenhauer the proposition that "life as representation alone, seen pure or reproduced in art, is a significant spectacle"—the proposition, that is, that life can be justified only as an aesthetic phenomenon. Life is art and appearance, nothing more, and therefore wisdom (as an affair of culture and life) stands higher than truth (which is a matter of morality). The wisdom meant is a tragically ironic one, which out of artistic instinct, for the sake of culture, holds science within bounds and defends life as the highest value on two fronts at once: against the pessimism of the calumniators of life, the apostles of an afterlife or of Nirvana; and against the optimism of the rationalists and reformers who preach their fables of justice and happiness on this earth for all men, and who prepare the way for a socialist uprising of the slaves. Nietzsche baptized this tragic wisdom, which accepts and blesses all the falsehood, harshness, and cruelty of life, with the name of Dionysus.

Invocation of the drunken god occurs first in the mystical aesthetic work of his youth, *The Birth of Tragedy from the Spirit of Music*, wherein the Dionysiac as an artistic and psychological state is opposed to Apollonian aloofness and objectivity as a principle of art. The polarity is very similar to that posited by Schiller in his famous essay on the "naïve" and the "sentimental." In *The Birth of Tragedy* Nietzsche for the first time uses the phrase "theoretical man," and assumes a combative posture toward Socrates, the archetype of this theoretical man; Socrates, the decrier of instinct, the glorifier of consciousness, who taught that only that which is conscious can be good, and who therefore must have been the enemy of Dionysus and the murderer of tragedy. Socrates, according to Nietzsche, is the father of an Alexandrian scientific culture, pallid, academic, inhospitable to myth and life; a culture which had nurtured optimism and rational religion; a culture of practical and theoretical utilitarianism which, like democracy itself, is a symptom of diminishing force and physiological weariness. The typical man of this Socratic, anti-tragic culture—theoretical man—no longer wants wholeness, with all the natural cruelty implicit in it; he has been enfeebled by the optimistic point of view. But, young Nietzsche prophesies, the age of Socratic man is past. A new race, heroic, intrepid, contemptuous of all doctrines of weakness, is entering the scene; a gradual awakening of the Dionysiac spirit can be observed in our contemporary world—the world of 1870. Out of the Dionysiac depths of the German spirit, of German music, of German philosophy, the rebirth of tragedy is taking place.

Later he desperately derided his onetime faith in the German spirit, and all he had attributed to it. For he had fashioned that German spirit completely in his own image. Its mildly humane, still sentimentally romantic character had been the character of the budding philosopher. His, too, was the universal perspective, the vision of Occidental culture as a whole, although he was still chiefly concerned with German *Kultur*, in whose lofty mission he trusted, for all that he saw it as terribly imperiled by Bismarck's establishment of a modern power state. Politics, democratic mediocratization, and the complacency of victory, he thought, would cause it to forfeit this mission. His brilliant diatribe against the smug and senile book by a theologian, David Friedrich Strauss, *Der alte und der neue Glaube* (*The Old and the New Religion*), was a savage criticism of the philistine complacency which threatened to rob the German spirit of all its depth. And even here, in so early a work, the youthful thinker cast prophetic glances ahead at his own destiny, which seemed to lie open before him like a tragic plan of life. I am referring to the passage in which he mocks at the ethical cowardice of Strauss, that commonplace apostle of Enlightenment. Strauss is very careful, he says, not to derive any life code from his Darwinian principles, from the *bellum omnium contra omnes*, the war of all against all and the right of the stronger to survive. He is an evolutionist only in so far as he lashes out against persons and miracles, aware that in this he will have the philistines on his side. Nietzsche already knows in the depths of his heart that he will do his utmost, not stopping short of madness, to infuriate the philistines.

The second volume of the *Thoughts Out of Season*, entitled "Of the Usefulness and Disadvantages of History for

Life," displays in almost finished form the outline of Nietzsche's fundamental idea, although still in the guise of criticism. This remarkable essay is at bottom a fugue taking for its
theme Hamlet's "Thus the native hue of resolution is sicklied
o'er with the pale cast of thought." The title is scarcely apt;
Nietzsche has little to say of the usefulness of history. On the
other hand, he makes much of its harmfulness to *life*, to precious, sacred, aesthetically justified life. The nineteenth century has been called the century of history, and in truth it
first produced and developed the sense of history, of which
earlier cultures (considered as cultures, as artistically coherent systems of life) knew little or nothing. Nietzsche actually speaks of the "historical disease" which, he alleges,
paralyzes life and spontaneity. Nowadays education is historical education, he maintains. The Greeks had known nothing of historical education; yet who would take it upon himself to call the Greeks uncultured? History pursued purely
for the sake of knowledge, not for purposes of life, and without the counterpoise of "shaping talent," of creative naïveté,
is murderous, is death. A historical phenomenon, once it is
throughly understood, is dead. A scientifically analyzed religion, for example, is done for, has reached its end. The
historico-critical treatment of Christianity—and here Nietzsche speaks like any conservative—reduces the religion to
mere knowledge about Christianity. In the course of historical examinations of religion things come to light which necessarily blast the devout mood of illusion which alone nour-
ishes the life of things. Man creates only when he loves,
when he is surrounded by the shadowy illusions of love. History must be manipulated like a work of art in order to serve
the creative ends of culture. But the analytical and anti-
artistic tendency of the age will not permit this. History ex-
pels the instincts. Educated, or miseducated, by history, man
can no longer "let the reins dangle" and act naïvely, trusting
in himself as the "divine animal." History always underesti-
mates the new things that are coming into being. It stultifies

action, which inevitably is irreverent toward the existing order. What history teaches and builds is *justice*. But life has no use for justice; life needs injustice, is essentially unjust. "It takes a great deal of strength," Nietzsche says, and we greatly wonder whether he attributed such strength to himself, "to be able to live and to forget to what extent living and being unjust are one and the same." But being able to forget is all that matters. He calls for the unhistorical point of view, for the art and the strength to forget and to enclose oneself in a limited horizon—a demand, we may add, easier to make than to fulfill. For though we are born with a limited horizon, to keep ourselves enclosed in it is aesthetic mummery and denial of fate, and is scarcely likely to yield anything genuine and decent. But Nietzsche, in his high-minded way, desires a suprahistorical point of view which will shift attention from the processes of growth to art and religion, which alone confer an eternal presentness upon existence. The enemy is positivistic science, for it recognizes only history and process, not the present and the eternal; science condemns forgetting as the death of knowledge, and seeks to abolish all limitations of horizon. But everything living requires a sheltering atmosphere, a mysterious aura, a cloak of delusion. A life governed by science is much less alive than one governed by instincts and powerful illusions. . . .

Nowadays the phrase "powerful illusions" reminds us of Sorel and his book *Sur la violence*, where no differentiation is yet made between proletarian syndicalism and fascism, and mass myth, quite independent of truth or falsehood, is pronounced the indispensable motive force of history. We ask ourselves, too, whether it would not be better to maintain in the masses respect for reason and truth, and in so doing honor their longing for justice—far better than to implant mass myths and turn loose upon mankind hordes dominated by "powerful illusions." Who does the latter nowadays, and to what ends? Certainly not for the glory of culture. But Nietzsche knows nothing about masses, and does not want to know about them. "The devil take them," he says, "them and statistics." The age he desires and prophesies is one in which men, unhistorically and suprahistorically, take care not to set up patterns for the universal process or even plot mankind's history; in which the masses are disregarded entirely and the only ones who count are the great men, those who are forever timelessly contemporary with one another, who above the milling turmoil of history hold their lofty intellectual converse with one another. The goal of humanity, he says, consists not in any ideal world order, but in its highest specimens. This is Nietzsche's individualism—an aesthetic cult of the genius and hero which he adopted from Schopenhauer along with the attitude that happiness is impossible, that the only possible and dignified course for man is a *heroic* life. Nietzsche's version of this concept, compounded with his adoration for the life of strength and beauty, results in a heroic aestheticism presided over by a patron saint—namely, the god of tragedy, Dionysus. This Dionysiac aestheticism later made of Nietzsche the greatest critic and psychologist of morality in the history of thought.

He was born to be a psychologist; psychology was his fundamental passion. Knowledge and psychology were for him at bottom one and the same passion; and it is indicative of the inner contradictoriness of this great and suffering mind that he who prized life far above knowledge gave himself so completely and irredeemably to psychology. He was a psychologist from the start by virtue of his allegiance to Schopenhauer's insight that the intellect does not engender the will, but vice versa; that the will, not the intellect, is the primary and dominant factor in the human psyche; that the intellect functions merely as a servant of the will. Intellect as the humble instrument of the will—that is the starting-point of all psychology, or, shall we say, of the psychology that suspects and unmasks human motives. And Nietzsche, as the advocate of life, throws himself into the arms of moral psychology; he suspects that all "good" impulses have their origin in bad

ones, and therefore proclaims the bad impulses to be the finer
ones which elevate life to a higher plane. That is his "revalu-
ation of all values."

All that he formerly called Socratism, "the theoretical
man," consciousness, the historical disease, he now lumps under the heading of "morality," especially "Christian morality." This he has now exposed as something thoroughly ven-
omous, rancorous, hostile to life. We must not forget that
Nietzsche's moral criticism is to some extent impersonal, an
attribute of his era. For around the turn of the century the
European intelligentsia was making its first head-on assault
upon the hypocritical morality of the middle-class Victorian
age. Nietzsche's furious war against morality fits to a considerable extent into the general picture, and there is often a
surprising family resemblance between his onslaughts and
those of others. It is certainly a surprise to observe the close
kinship of many of Nietzsche's *aperçus* with the far from
vain tilts against morality with which, at approximately the
same time, Oscar Wilde was shocking and amusing his public. When Wilde declares: "For, try as we may, we cannot
get behind the appearance of things to reality. And the terrible reason may be that there is no reality in things apart
from their experiences"; when he speaks of the "truth of
masks" and the "decay of the lie"; when he bursts out: "To
me beauty is the wonder of wonders. It is only shallow people who do not judge by appearances. The true mystery of
the world is the visible, not the invisible"; when he calls
truth something so personal that the same truth can never be
recognized by two different minds; when he says: "Every
impulse that we strive to strangle broods in the mind and
poisons us. . . . The only way to get rid of a temptation is
to yield to it"; and: "Don't be led astray into the paths of
virtue!"—we cannot help seeing that all these quotations
might have come from Nietzsche. And when, on the other
hand, we find Nietzsche saying: "Earnestness, that unmistakable sign of slow metabolism"; or: "In art lies are hallowed

and the will to deception has a clear conscience on its side";
or: "We are basically inclined to maintain that the falsest
judgments are the most indispensable to us"; or: "It is only
moral prejudice to assert that truth is more valuable than appearance"—there is not one of these sentences which could
not have occurred in Wilde's comedies and have earned a
laugh in the St. James's Theatre. Those critics who ranked
Wilde high compared his plays with Sheridan's *The School
for Scandal*. Much that Nietzsche wrote seems to have come
out of this school.

Of course there is something almost sacrilegious about the
juxtaposition of Nietzsche and Wilde, for the latter was a
dandy, the German philosopher a kind of saint of immoralism. And yet the more or less sought-after martyrdom at the
end of Wilde's life—Reading Gaol—adds to his dandyism a
touch of sanctity which would have aroused Nietzsche's full
sympathy. What reconciled Nietzsche ultimately to Socrates was the end, the cup of hemlock. He held that this martyr's death had made an inestimable impression upon Greek
youth and upon Plato. Similarly, he excepted the person of
Jesus of Nazareth from his hatred for historical Christianity,
again on account of the end, the crucifixion which he loved
to the depths of his being, and to which he himself willingly
submitted.

His life was inebriation and suffering—a highly artistic
combination. In mythological terms, it was the union of Dionysus with the Crucified One. Swinging the thyrsus, he sang
hymns to strength and beauty, the amoral triumph of life. He
defended life against all the mind's attempts to cripple it—
and at the same time paid unexampled homage to suffering.
"Place in the hierarchy," he said, "is determined by how
deeply a person can suffer." These are not the words of an
antimoralist. Nor is there any element of antimoralism in
his pronouncement: "As far as pain and renunciation are concerned, my life during my last years matches that of every
ascetic of any age." He wrote this with pride, not asking for

sympathy. "I want my life to be as hard as it is possible for a man's to be." He made it hard for himself, hard to the point of sanctity, for Schopenhauer's saint always remained for him the exemplar of the highest type of man, and his conception of the heroic career was the career of the saint. What makes the saint? That he does none of the things he would like to do, and all the things he does not like. That is how Nietzsche lived: "Renouncing all I respected, renouncing even respect itself. . . . Thou shalt be master of thyself, master even of thine own virtues." This is the "stunt of overleaping oneself" of which Novalis once spoke, and which he declared to be the supreme feat of all. This "stunt"—the term is drawn from the world of acrobats and trapeze artists—has in Nietzsche none of the acrobat's gay virtuosity, none of the dancer's joyousness. All the "dancelike" elements in his conduct were the paroxysms of the will, and entailed pain. In overleaping himself he was bloodily cutting his own flesh, practicing flagellation, moralism. His concept of truth was in itself ascetic; for to him truth was what hurts, and he would distrust any truth that gave him ease. "Among the forces which nourished morality was truth," he says; "truth finally turned against morality, discovered its aims, what it had at stake. . . ." His "immoralism," then, was the self-destruction of morality out of concern for truth. But he hints that this is a kind of excess and luxuriance on the part of morality, for he speaks of morality's hereditary wealth which allows it to be spendthrift and throw a great deal out of the window without particularly impoverishing itself.

All these ideas stand back of the atrocities and the drunken messages of power, violence, cruelty, and political trickery into which his idea of life as a work of art, and of an unreflective culture governed by instinct, degenerated so brilliantly in his later writings. When a critic once wrote that Nietzsche was pleading for the abolition of all decent feelings, the misunderstood philosopher was utterly baffled. "Much obliged!" he said scornfully. For he had conceived it all in a highly respectable and humanitarian sense, in the sense of a higher, more profound, prouder, finer sort of human race. He had, so to speak, not "meant anything by it"— not anything bad, at any rate, although he would not deny that he had meant to be spiteful. For everything profound is spiteful; life itself is profoundly spiteful; it is not cut along the lines of morality; it knows nothing about "truth"; it rests upon appearances and artistic lies; it mocks at virtue, for it is in essence ruthlessness and exploitation. And, says Nietzsche, there is a pessimism of strength, an intellectual predilection for the harsh, the fearful, the spiteful, the problematical aspects of existence. This predilection springs from well-being, from fullness of being. The euphoric syphilitic ascribes this "well-being," this "fullness of being" to himself, and makes it his business to proclaim that those aspects of life hitherto negated, negated especially by Christianity, are the very ones most deserving affirmation. Life *über alles!* Why? He never said why. He never suggested any reason why life should be unconditionally worshipped and regarded as supremely worth preserving. He merely proclaimed that living is superior to knowing, for in destroying life cognition destroys itself. Life is the prerequisite to knowing, and therefore cognition must be concerned with it in the interests of self-preservation. In other words, there must be life if anything is to be known.

It seems to us, however, that this logic does not suffice to account for Nietzsche's enthusiastic advocacy of life. If he were to see "life" as the creation of a god, there would be a validity to his reverence, even though we personally should find little reason to bow in the dust before the exploding universe of modern physics. But in fact he sees life as a massive and senseless excrescence of the will to power, and demands that we hail with delight its very senselessness and colossal amorality. His salute is not "Hosannah!" but "Evoe!" and the cry has an extraordinarily broken and tormented ring. For his dogma denied that there is something in man beyond mere biology, some margin of spirit not completely absorbed by interest in life, some possibility of stepping outside this interest, a form of critical detachment which is perhaps the same thing that Nietzsche calls "morality," and which can never seriously affect good old life—life being far too unregenerate for that—but which may act as a gentle corrective, may hone man's conscience somewhat, as Christianity has always done. "There is no fixed point outside of life," Nietzsche says, "from which it would be possible to reflect upon existence; there is no authority before which life might be ashamed." Really not? We have the feeling that there is one after all, and if it is not morality, then it is simply the spirit of man, humanity itself assuming the form of criticism, irony and freedom, allied with the judging word. "Life has no judge above itself." Really not? In man nature and life somehow go beyond themselves; in him they lose their innocence. They acquire *mind*—and mind is life's self-criticism. This humane something in us throws a pitiful glance at Nietzsche's "hygienic doctrine" of life. In his saner days it was the disease of historicism against which that doctrine contended, but as time went on it became a maenadic rage against truth, morality, religion, humanitarianism, against everything that might effect a reasonable taming of life's savagery.

As far as I see, there are two prime errors which deranged Nietzsche's thinking and gave it its fatal cast. The first was a total and, we must assume, willful misinterpretation of the relative power of instinct and intellect on this earth. It seems to have been his notion that intellect is dangerously dominant, is on the point of overwhelming instinct, so that instinct must be saved from it. When we consider how completely, in the great majority of men, will, instinct, and selfishness dominate and repress intellect, reason, and sense of justice, it is evidently absurd to believe that instinct must be given the upper hand. That belief can be explained only in historical terms, as arising out of a momentary situation in philosophy, as a corrective of rationalistic smugness; and as soon as the correction is made, a countercorrection is needed. As if it were really necessary to defend life against mind! As if there were the slightest danger of too much intellectualism on earth! Elementary fairness should counsel us to cherish and protect the feeble little flame of reason, intellect, and justice, not join sides with power and the instinctual life and riotously whoop it up for negatives, for every sort of criminality. In our contemporary world we have seen the folly of this. Nietzsche did a great deal of mischief by acting as if man's moral consciousness were a devil threatening life, like Mephistopheles, with a cold diabolic fist. For my part, I see nothing especially diabolic in the thought (an old idea of the mystics) that life may someday be abolished by the human spirit—there is a good while, a vast good while, to wait before that ever comes about. Far more pressing is the danger that life on this planet may abolish itself by means of the atom bomb. But that, too, is unlikely. Life is a cat with many lives, and so is humanity.

The second of Nietzsche's errors is the utterly false relationship into which he puts life and morality when he treats them as antagonists. The truth is that they belong together. Ethics is the prop of life, and the moral man a true citizen of life's realm—perhaps a somewhat boring fellow, but highly useful. The real dichotomy lies between ethics and aesthetics. Not morality, but beauty is allied to death, as many poets have said and sung. How could Nietzsche not know this? "When Socrates and Plato began to speak of truth and justice," he says at one time, "they were no longer Greeks, but Jews—or I do not know what." Well, the Jews, thanks to their morality, have proved themselves good and persevering children of life. They have, along with their religion, their belief in a just God, survived millennia, while the profligate little nation of aesthetes and artists, the Greeks, vanished very quickly from the stage of history.

But Nietzsche, quite removed from all racist anti-Semitism, sees in Judaism the cradle of Christianity, while in the latter

he finds, quite rightly but with abhorrence, the germ of democracy, of the French Revolution, and of hated "modern
ideas," which he brands scathingly as herd morality. "Shop-
keepers, Christians, cows, females, Englishmen and other
democrats," he says; for he sees England as the source of
"modern ideas" (the French, he avers, were only the soldiers of the ideas). And what he despises and reviles in these
modern ideas is their utilitarianism and eudaemonism, their
elevation of peace and happiness on earth to the supreme de-
siderata—whereas the aristocratic, the heroic and tragic man
spurns such common and feeble values. This heroic man is
necessarily a warrior, hard toward himself and others, ready
to sacrifice himself and others. His chief quarrel with Christianity is that it has raised individuals to such importance that
they can no longer be sacrificed. But, says Nietzsche, the species survives only by human sacrifice, and Christianity is in
principle the counterpoise to natural selection. It has reduced
and enfeebled the strength, the responsibility, the high obligation to sacrifice human beings, and for thousands of years,
down to the appearance of Nietzsche himself, has checked
that forward movement which, "by breeding on the one
hand and by the annihilation of millions of misbegotten creatures on the other, shapes the future man and is not daunted
by the unprecedented suffering it engenders." Who in recent
times have had the strength to undertake this responsibility,
who have dared to ascribe this greatness to themselves, and
who have unswervingly fulfilled the high obligation by sacrificing hecatombs of human beings? A gang of megalomani-
acal petty bourgeois, the very sight of whom would have
nauseated Nietzsche.

But that was not within his experience. Nor did he experience any war after the old-fashioned breech-loader war of
1870. Consequently, out of sheer aversion to the Christian
and democratic striving for happiness and love of mankind,
he could extol war in a manner which sounds to us today like
the jabber of an excited boy. That a good cause justifies war

is far too moralistic a sentiment for him; rather, he would have a good war justify *any* cause. "Nowadays," he writes, "the evaluation of various forms of society is identical with evaluation of peace as of greater worth than war; but this judgment is antibiological, is itself the spawn of life's decadence. . . . Life is an outgrowth of war; society itself is an instrument of war." It does not occur to him that it might not be a bad thing if we tried to make of society something other than an instrument of war. For him society is a product of nature and so once again is based on amoral premises. To tamper with these premises would amount to a malignant attack upon life itself. "To renounce war is to renounce the grandeur of life itself," he cries out. Of life and of culture, he develops the argument; for culture can only be renewed by strong doses of barbarism, and it is vain sentimentalism to expect anything in the way of culture and greatness from men if they have forgotten how to wage war. He himself despises all nationalistic stupidity. But this emotion is plainly a prerogative of special individuals, for he describes outbursts of nationalistic mania for power and sacrifice with an enthusiasm which leaves no doubt that he would want to keep the "powerful illusion" of nationalism for the masses.

A comment is essential at this point. We have learned by experience that in some circumstances unconditional pacifism can be a more than questionable, a treacherous and pernicious affair. For years pacifism hung over Europe and the world as nothing but the mask for fascist sympathies. True friends of peace felt that the peace of Munich, which the democracies concluded with fascism in 1938 allegedly to spare the nations of the world the horrors of war, was the nadir of European history. The war against Hitler, or rather the mere readiness to make war against him—which would have sufficed—was desired by those friends of peace. But when we see—and how can we not see?—the destruction, ruin, and corruption engendered by even a war waged for humanity, the demoralization, the unleashing of every brutal, selfish, and

antisocial instinct; when we project what we have recently
undergone to form an approximate picture of this earth after
a next, a third world war—then Nietzsche's rhapsodies on the
selective and culture-saving function of war strike us as the
fantasies of an inexperienced child, offspring of a long era of
peace and blue-chip security which was beginning to bore.

Since he also predicted, with amazing prophetic flair, a
succession of monstrous wars and cataclysms, veritably the
classic age of war, "to which posterity will look back with
envy and reverence," the humanitarian degeneration and cas-
tration of mankind had evidently not progressed so dangerously far. It is hard, therefore, to see why the human race
should need to be spurred on to the selective slaughter by
philosophy also. Was the aim of this philosophy to dispose of
the moral scruples which might stand in the way of the coming horrors? Was it to whip mankind into shape for the magnificent contest? If so, it applies itself to the matter with a
voluptuous zest which does not so much shock us—it was intended to shock—as it alarms us for the sanity of the noble
mind which is here raging so lustfully against itself. For he
goes disturbingly beyond mere education toward manliness
when he lists, describes, and recommends medieval forms of
torture with a sensual enjoyment whose mark is still to be
found in contemporary German literature. It borders on vi-
ciousness when "as comfort to milksops" he asks us to consider the capacity for pain of lower races, say the Negroes.
And when the hymn to the "blond beast" begins, to "the ex-
ultant monster," the type of man who "returns home from
an atrocious series of murders, burnings, rapes, and tortures
as high-spiritedly as though coming from a student's prank"
—then the clinical picture of infantile sadism is complete, and
our souls writhe in embarrassment.

The romantic poet Novalis—a spiritual kinsman of Nietzsche, that is—delivered the most trenchant criticism of this
attitude. "The ideal of morality," he says, "has no more dangerous rival than the ideal of supreme strength, of a life of

maximum vigor, which has also been called the ideal of aesthetic greatness. That life is in truth the ultimate attainment of the barbarian, and unfortunately in these days of civilization's withering it has won a great many adherents. In pursuance of this ideal man becomes a hybrid thing, a brute-spirit, whose cruel mentality exerts a horrible spell upon weaklings."

The matter could not have been stated better. Was Nietzsche familiar with this passage? He must have been. But he would not let it hinder him in his drunken baiting of the "ideal of morality"—his drunkenness was deliberate and therefore his challenges were not really intended seriously. What Novalis called the ideal of aesthetic greatness, the ultimate attainment of the barbarian, man as brute-spirit, is nothing more nor less than Nietzsche's superman. Nietzsche defines him thus: the "crystallization out of a superior minority, in which a stronger species, a higher type, comes to light, whose conditions for genesis and survival differ from those of the average man." This is the future master of the earth; this is the resplendent tyrant type. Democracy is just good enough to produce him. Once present, he will use democracy as a tool, will with Machiavellian craft introduce his new morality by attaching it to the existing moral code, casting it into the language of that code. For this terrifying utopia of greatness, strength, and beauty by far prefers lies to the truth—since lying requires superior mentality and will. The superman is the man "in whom the specific qualities of life—injustice, deceit, exploitation—are at their greatest."

It would be pointlessly harsh to respond to all these shrill, tormented challenges with scorn and abuse—and sheer stupidity to respond with moral indignation. What we see before us is a Hamlet figure, the tragedy of insight exceeding strength, and our feelings should be those of awe and pity. "I believe," Nietzsche said once, "that I have guessed some secrets of the highest man's soul. Perhaps everyone who guesses them is destroyed." He was destroyed by his understanding.

And the grotesqueries of his doctrine are so permeated by infinitely moving lyrical grief, by such painful longing for the dew of love to fall on the parched, rainless land of his solitude, that any scorn or repugnance we may feel for his *Ecce homo* is quickly checked.

But we are in a bit of a dilemma when socialism—which Nietzsche denounced a hundred times over as the poisonous opponent of the higher life and contemptuously termed "the movement of the subjugated caste"—tells us that his superman is nothing but idealization of the fascist leader. He himself with all his philosophizing, we are told, was nothing but the forerunner, co-creator, and ideologue of European and world fascism. I personally am inclined to reverse cause and effect in this matter. I would say not that Nietzsche created fascism, but that fascism created him. That is to say, this non-political and at bottom innocent intellectual was so delicate a recording instrument that he sensed the rise of imperialism and the fascist era of the Occident, in which we are now living and will be living for a long time, in spite of the military victory over fascism. Nietzsche, with his philosophic creed of power, was like a quivering needle pointing to the future.

As a thinker who from the start had broken completely with all that smacked of the bourgeoisie, he apparently accepted the fascist components of the post-bourgeois era and rejected the socialist elements for the reason that the latter were moral and Nietzsche was prone to confuse morality in general with bourgeois morality. But with his sensitivity he could not fail to register the influence of socialist elements upon the future; and this is what the socialists overlook when they condemn him as a fascist pure and simple. The question is not in fact so uncomplicated—for all that it may seem so. His heroic contempt for happiness was a highly personal matter and scarcely applicable to the political scene. True, this contempt misled him into condemning as "the green-pasture happiness of herd animals" all efforts to eliminate the most shameful social and economic abuses and to diminish avoidable suffering on earth. Not for nothing was his phrase "the dangerous life" translated into Italian and incorporated into the argot of fascism. All his ranting against morality, humanity, pity, and Christianity, all his diseased enthusiasm for sublime amorality, war, and evil, unfortunately had its place in the trashy ideology of fascism. Aberrations such as his "morality for physicians," with recommendations that the sick be liquidated and the inferior castrated, his insistence on the necessity of slavery, and a good many of his eugenic ideas about selection, breeding, and marriage in the interests of racial hygiene, were actually incorporated into the theory and practice of Nazism—though perhaps without conscious reference to him. If it is true that "By their fruits ye shall know them," Nietzsche's case is lost. In the work of Spengler, his clever imitator, the *Herrenmensch* of Nietzsche's dreams becomes the modern "man of action," a predatory profiteer who marches over corpses, a financial magnate, armaments-manufacturer—the type of the German industrialist who financed fascism. In short, Spengler obtusely represents Nietzsche as the philosophical spokesman of imperialism—which in reality Nietzsche did not understand at all. How otherwise could he have expressed his contempt all down the line for the commercial, shopkeeping spirit, which he considered pacifistic, and which he countered by praising the spirit of the soldierly life? With his "aristocratic radicalism" he did not see that imperialism consists in the political union of industrialism and militarism, and that it is the spirit of commercialism which makes wars.

Let us not deceive ourselves. Fascism as a mousetrap for the masses, as the most shameless rabble-rousing and the lowest sort of cultural vulgarism history has ever known, could only have been alien to the spirit of the man for whom everything revolved on the question: "What is aristocratic?" He could not even have imagined such a phenomenon as fascism. And that the German middle class confounded the onslaught of the Nazis with Nietzsche's dreams of a barbarism that would renew civilization—this was the crudest of misunderstandings. I am not speaking of his disdain for chauvinism, his hatred of the German Reich and of obscurantist German power politics, his European point of view, his scorn for anti-Semitism and the rotten lies of racism. But I reiterate that the socialistic element in his vision of life after the bourgeois era was just as strong as the element which has been called fascist. What else is it when Zarathustra cries: "I implore you, my brethren, remain faithful to the earth! No longer hide your head in the sand of heavenly things, but bear it free and erect, an earthly head which creates meanings for this earth. . . . Like me, bring strayed virtue back to earth, yea, back to love and life, so that she may give a meaning to earth, a human meaning." This is the urge to permeate material things with human spirit. It is spiritual materialism—which is socialism.

His concept of culture has in places a strongly socialistic cast, or, at any rate, a no longer bourgeois hue. He was against the growing gulf between the cultured and the uncultured, and his youthful Wagnerism was primarily a battle cry against the Renaissance trimmings of the great age of the German bourgeoisie. He wanted an art for high and low, no more of those sophisticated pleasures which do not speak to the hearts of all men.

It is evidence not of hostility toward workers, but of the opposite when he says: "The workers ought to learn to think of themselves as soldiers; they should receive an honorarium, a salary, but no wages. Someday they ought to live as the bourgeois do now; but above them, distinguishing themselves by their frugality; they should be the higher caste, therefore poorer and simpler, but in possession of the power." And he gave strange instructions for making property more moral: "Let all the avenues of work that lead to moderate enrichment be kept open," he says, "but effortless, sudden wealth should be prevented. All the branches of transportation and

commerce which are favorable to the accumulation of great
fortunes, especially finance, should be taken out of the hands
of private persons and private corporations. The possessors
of too much and of nothing should be equally regarded as
dangers to the community." The idea that the possessor of
nothing is a dangerous beast stems from Schopenhauer, the
philosopher with a bank account; that the possessor of too
much is dangerous was an idea contributed by Nietzsche
himself.

Around 1875, more than seventy years ago, he prophesied
a European League of Nations "in which each individual nation, its borders defined by geographical utility, will occupy
the position of a canton with similar special privileges." He
felt no special fervor for this arrangement, but saw it simply
as the consequence of victorious democracy. The point is
that his perspective at that time was purely European. In the
course of the following decade it expanded into a global and
universal vision. He speaks of the inevitable organization of
the total economy of the globe as impending. He calls for as
many as possible international agencies—"in order to practice
a world-wide perspective." His faith in Europe wavers. "At
bottom the Europeans imagine that they now represent the
superior man on this earth. The people of Asia are a hundred
times more glorious than the Europeans." On the other hand,
he fancies that in the world of the future spiritual influence
may remain with the typical European, who by synthesis out
of the European past will become the supreme type of intellectual man. "The dominion of the earth—Anglo-Saxon. The
German element—a good ferment; the Germans do not know
how to rule." Then again he sees an intermixture of the German and Slavic races, and Germany as an advance post of
Slavism, preparing the way for a pan-Slavic Europe. He is
quite clear about the rise of Russia as a world power: "Power
divided between Slavs and Anglo-Saxons, and a Europe like
Greece under the domination of Rome."

These are startling conclusions indeed to have been garnered from a casual survey of the domain of world politics, undertaken by a mind fundamentally concerned only with culture's duty to breed philosophers, artists, and saints. He sees, across the span of nearly a century, approximately what we see today. For the world, the newly forming view of the world, is a unity; and wherever a mind of such extraordinary sensitivity turns, in whatever direction it reaches out with its pseudopodia, it feels whatever is new, whatever is to come. Purely intuitively, Nietzsche anticipates the conclusions of modern physics in his assault upon the mechanistic interpretation of the universe, in his denial of a causally determined world, in his rejection of the classical "natural law" of the recurrence of identical cases. "There is no second time." He denies predictability: that a particular effect need necessarily follow a particular cause. The cause-and-effect interpretation of events is false, he holds. What takes place is rather a struggle between two elements of unequal force, and a new arrangement of forces in which the new state is something basically different from the old, and by no means the effect of the old state. Nietzsche's point of view, that is, is dynamic rather than logical and mechanical. His "premonitions in natural science," to borrow Helmholtz's phrase about Goethe, have a distinct intellectual bias. They aim at something; they accord with his tenets on power, with his antirationalism, and further support him in his elevation of life above law— there being something "moral" and therefore hateful about law as such. But, for all that he had an axe to grind—as far as science is concerned, he has turned out to be right, for physics has meanwhile reduced "law" to mere probability and drifted away from the concept of causality.

As with all his thinking, in his ideas on physics he stepped out of the bourgeois world of classical rationality into a new world in which he himself, by virtue of his origins, was a complete foreigner. Socialists who refuse to account that in his favor are apt to say that he himself belonged far more to the bourgeois world than he knew.

A revision is due in the theory that Nietzsche was a writer of aphorisms without any central core to his thinking. His philosophy is quite as much a thoroughly organized system as Schopenhauer's. It evolves out of a single fundamental idea which pervades the whole of it. But this starting-point is, it must be granted, of a starkly aesthetic sort—which in itself would place his vision and thought in irreconcilable opposition to all socialist doctrine. In the final analysis there are only two basic attitudes, two points of view: the aesthetic and the moral. Socialism is a strictly moral world-view. Nietzsche, on the other hand, is the most uncompromisingly perfect aesthete in the history of thought. His major premise, which contains within itself his Dionysiac pessimism—namely, that life can be justified only as an aesthetic phenomenon—applies exactly to himself, to his life, his thinking, and his writing. These can be justified, understood, honored, only as an aesthetic phenomenon. Consciously, down to his self-mythologizing in his last moment, down to madness, this life was an artistic production, not only in terms of its wonderful expressiveness, but in terms of its innermost nature. It was a lyric, tragic spectacle, and one of utmost fascination.

It is curious, although comprehensible, that aestheticism was the first manifestation of the European mind's rebellion against the whole morality of the bourgeois age. Not for nothing have I coupled the names of Nietzsche and Wilde—they belong together as rebels, rebels in the name of beauty, for all that the German iconoclast's rebellion went tremendously deeper and cost tremendously more in suffering, renunciation, and self-conquest. I have read socialist critics, particularly among the Russians, who declare that although Nietzsche's aesthetic perceptions and judgments are often of admirable subtlety, he was only a barbarian in his political ethics. This view is too pat, in so far as it fails to see that Nietzsche's glorification of barbarism is simply an excess of his aesthetic drunkenness. In any case, here is a close relationship which we have every reason to ponder: that of aestheticism and barbarism. Toward the end of the nineteenth century the ill-omened proximity of these two was not yet seen, felt, or feared. For if it had been, Georg Brandes, a liberal writer and a Jew, could not have brought himself to discover a new nuance in the German philosopher's "aristocratic radicalism"—and to give proselytizing lectures on the matter. That he did so is a sign of the sense of security which still prevailed at that time, of the insouciance of the declining bourgeois age. But it is a sign, too, that the clever Danish critic did not take Nietzsche's barbarism seriously, did not take it at its word, but with a grain of salt—in which he was perfectly right.

For something spurious, irresponsible, unreliable, and passionately frivolous existed within these philosophical effusions. That something was an element of deepest irony which thwarts the understanding of the simpler reader. Nietzsche's aestheticism, his raging denial of intellect in favor of the beauty, strength, and wickedness of life—was, in fact, the self-lashing of a man who suffered profoundly from life. What Nietzsche offers is not only art—a special art is required to read him, and in reading him literalness and straightforwardness are of no avail. Rather, cunning, irony, reserve are requisite. Anyone who takes Nietzsche "as he is," who believes him and takes him at his word, is lost. Seneca, Nietzsche said, is a man to whom we must always lend our ears but never our loyalty or belief. So it stands with Nietzsche. Are examples necessary? The reader of *The Case of Wagner* can scarcely trust his eyes when in a letter from Nietzsche to Carl Fuchs, the musician, written in 1888, he suddenly sees: "What I say about Bizet you must not take seriously; for my taste, Bizet simply does not count at all. But as an ironic antithesis to Wagner it is extremely effective. . . ." So much—"between ourselves"—for the glowing eulogy of *Carmen* in *The Case of Wagner*. This is startling, but it is not the half of it. In another letter to Fuchs, Nietzsche coaches his friend on how best to write about him as a psychologist, writer, and immoralist. The critic should not judge for or against him, but should characterize him with neutrality. "It is completely unnecessary, and even undersirable, to take my side. On the contrary, a dose of curiosity mingled with ironical resistance, as of someone confronted with a strange plant, would seem to be a far more intelligent attitude toward me. —Forgive me! I have just written a few naïve remarks—a little recipe for getting yourself happily out of an impossible situation. . . ."

Has any writer ever warned against himself in so strange a manner? "Antiliberal to the point of malice," he calls himself. Antiliberal out of malice, out of perversity, would have been a more correct description. When the hundred-day Kaiser, Frederick III, the liberal with English marital ties, died in 1888, Nietzsche was as moved and downcast as all the German liberals. "At last there was a faint glimmering of free thought, the last hope for Germany. Now the reign of Stöcker begins. I draw the logical conclusion and know already that my *Will to Power* will be banned in Germany first of all. . . ." He was wrong, it was not banned. The spirit of the liberal era was still too strong; it was still possible to say anything in Germany. In Nietzsche's mourning for Frederick, however, something very simple, plain, and unparadoxical unexpectedly comes to light. The truth comes to light, if you will—the natural love of the intellectual, of the writer, for freedom, which is the air he breathes. And suddenly the whole aesthetic phantasm of slavery, war, violence, glorious brutality whisks itself off to a realm of irresponsible play and scintillating theory.

All his life Nietzsche pronounced curses upon the "theoretical man," but he himself was this theoretical man *par excellence*. His thinking was sheer virtuosity, unpragmatic in the extreme, untinged by any sense of pedagogic responsibility, profoundly unpolitical. It was in truth without relationship to life, to that beloved life which he defended and hailed above all else. He never troubled himself in the slightest as to how his doctrines would work out in practice, in political reality. Nor did any of the ten thousand apostles of irrationality who in his shadow sprang like mushrooms out of the ground all over Germany. No wonder. For nothing could be more convenient to the German situation than his aesthetic theoreticism. As a matter of fact, he also hurled his sulphurous critical thunderbolts at the Germans, those corrupters of European history, and left them with not a hair unsinged. But who, in the end, was more German than he; who served the Germans as still another model for those traits which made them a disaster and terror to the world, and led them ultimately to ruin themselves: romantic passion; the drive to eternal expansion of the self into space, without any fixed object; will which is free because it has no goal and aspires to the infinite? Interestingly enough, Nietzsche called drunkenness and the tendency to suicide the peculiar vices of the Germans. Their great danger, he said, lay in everything that cribbed the forces of reason and unleashed the emotions, for "the emotions of Germans are directed against their own good and are as self-destructive as the drunkard's. Even enthusiasm means less in Germany than elsewhere, for it is unfruitful." What does Zarathustra call himself? "Knower of himself, hangman of himself."

In more than one sense Nietzsche has become historic. He made history, frightful history, and did not exaggerate when he called himself "a nemesis." For aesthetic effect he made too great a point of the solitude. In fact he belongs, although in a pronouncedly German form, to a general movement in the West comprising such figures as Kierkegaard, Bergson, and many others, a movement of intellectual revolt against the classical faith in reason of the eighteenth and nineteenth centuries. It has done its work—or, rather, all that still remains is the reconstitution of human reason upon a new basis, the achievement of a concept of humanity of greater profundity than the complacently shallow view of the bourgeois age.

The defense of instinct against reason and consciousness

was a corrective needed at a given time. But permanently, eternally necessary is the correction of life by mind—or by morality, if you will. How time-bound, how theoretic and inexperienced, Nietzsche's romanticizing of evil seems to us today. We have made the acquaintance of evil in all its nauseating forms, and are no longer such aesthetes that we need to be ashamed of subscribing to the good, nor need to snub such trivial ideas and guides as truth, freedom, justice. In the final analysis aestheticism, under whose banner freethinkers turned against bourgeois morality, itself belonged to the bourgeois age. And to go beyond this age means to step out of an aesthetic era into a moral and social one. An aesthetic ideology is absolutely unempowered to meet the problems we must solve—this is the plain fact, foɪ all that Nietzsche's genius had so much to do with creating the new atmosphere.

At one time he hazarded the thought that in the future world of his vision religious forces might still be strong enough to build an atheistic religion like Buddha's, which would brush aside sectarian differences. And he thought science would have no quarrel with such a new ideal. "But," he hastens to add, "this will not be general love of mankind." What if it were? It need not take the form of that optimistic, idyllic love of "the human race" which caused hearts to throb in the eighteenth century—and to which, incidentally, ethics owes tremendous progress. Yet when Nietzsche proclaimed: "God is dead"—a conclusion which cost him in particular unspeakably dear—in whose honor and for whose elevation was he doing this, if not for man's? If he was an atheist, if he was able to be one, he was so out of love for mankind—foolishly idyllic though these words may sound. He will have to bear with being called a humanist, just as he must bear with our interpreting his criticism of morality as a last offshoot of the Enlightenment. I cannot conceive of the supradenominational religion of which he speaks as other than allied to the humanitarian ideal, a religiously based and colored humanism which, out of depths of experience, having survived many trials, includes all knowledge of the lower and daemonic elements of man's nature in its homage to the mystery of man.

Religion is reverence—reverence first of all for the riddle which man is. Where what we really need is a new order, new relationships, the recasting of society to meet the global demands of the hour, certainly little can be done by conference decisions, technical measures, legal institutions. World government remains a rationalistic utopia. The main thing is a transformation of the spiritual climate, a new feeling for the difficulty and the nobility of being human, an all-pervasive fundamental disposition shared by everyone, and acknowledged by everyone within himself as the supreme judge. To the genesis and establishment of that disposition poets and artists, imperceptibly working through the depth and breadth of society, can make some contribution. But it is not something that can be taught and created; it must be experienced and suffered.

Philosophy is not a cold abstraction, but consists of experiencing, suffering, and sacrificing for humanity. This Nietzsche knew and demonstrated. In so doing, he was driven upward to the snow-covered peaks of grotesque error; but the future was truly the land he loved, and to coming generations he will stand, as he did to us who in our youth owed so much to him, a frail and honorably tragic figure illumined by the lightnings of these times of upheaval.

Translated by Richard and Clara Winston

CHEKHOV

WHEN Anton Chekhov died of tuberculosis of the lungs in Badenweiler in July 1904, I was a young man who had entered the literary field with a few stories and one novel which owed a good deal to the narrative art of nineteenth-century Russia. Yet I have tried in vain today to recall the impression made upon me at the time by the death of the Russian writer only fifteen years older than myself. I can remember nothing. The announcement in the German press must have left me rather unmoved. And no doubt whatever was written about Chekhov on that occasion had failed to deepen my awareness of this man who had died too early for Russia, too early for the world. Very likely these obituaries testified to the same ignorance that determined my own attitude to the life and work of this author, an attitude that was to change but slowly with the years.

What were the reasons for this ignorance? In my case it may be partly explained by my admiration for the "great work," the "long wind," the monumental epic sustained and completed by the power of unyielding patience, by my worship of the mighty creators like Balzac, Tolstoy, Wagner, whom it was my dream to emulate if I could. And Chekhov, like Maupassant, whose work incidentally I knew much better, expressed himself in the more restricted form, in the short story, which did not require years or a decade of heroic perseverance but could be tossed off by literary lightweights in a matter of days or weeks. For this medium I felt a certain scorn, little realizing what inner depth the short and concise can acquire in the hands of genius; how brevity, by embracing the whole fullness of life, can rise to a positively epic level, can even surpass in artistic intensity works of monumental stature, which are bound occasionally to flag, to lapse into a venerable dullness. If in later life I understood this fact better than in my youth, it was due mainly to my preoccupation with Chekhov's narrative art, which is unsurpassed in European literature.

To speak in more general terms, I feel that Chekhov was underestimated for so many years in western Europe, and even in Russia, on account of his extremely sober, critical, and doubting attitude toward himself, above all toward his own work—in a word, on account of his *modesty*, which, however endearing a virtue, was not conducive to making the world consider him great and important; indeed, it could be said that by this modesty he set the world a bad example. For the opinion we have of ourselves is not without influence on the picture other men paint of us; it colors their ideas, sometimes even distorts them. This short-story writer remained too long convinced of the insignificance of his talent, of his artistic unworthiness. He acquired some faith in himself, the faith that is essential if others are to believe in us, only by degrees and very painfully. To the end he had nothing of the literary *grand seigneur* about him, still less of the sage or prophet of Tolstoy, who looked benignly down on him and, according to Gorky, saw in him "an excellent, quiet, *modest* fellow."

Coming from a man whose immodesty was no less colossal than Wagner's, such praise is a trifle surprising. No doubt Chekhov would have accepted it with a polite, ironical smile; for politeness, dutiful veneration tinged with irony, set the tone of his relations with the giant from Yasnaya Polyana. Occasionally, not of course face to face with the overwhelming personality but in letters to a third person, this irony broke into open rebellion. On his return from his "descent into hell," his trying journey to the penal island of Sakhalin,

Chekhov wrote: "What a dull, sour fellow I should be today had I remained between my four walls! Before this journey, for instance, I considered Tolstoy's *Kreutzer Sonata* an important event; now it strikes me as comical and absurd." Tolstoy's imperial—as well as questionable—prophetic airs irritated him. "To the devil with the philosophy of the mighty ones of this world!" he wrote. "All great sages are as despotic as generals, and as rude as generals, convinced as they are of impunity." This gibe was provoked by Tolstoy's denunciation of doctors as useless scoundrels. For Chekhov himself was a doctor, a man dedicated to his profession, and he believed science to be one of the forces making for progress, to be an enemy of disgraceful human conditions, since it enlightened both heads and hearts. The wisdom of "oppose no evil," of "passive resistance," the contempt for culture and progress in which the great man indulged, appeared to Chekhov as so much reactionary twaddle. However great a man may be, he has no business laying down the law on topics of which he is totally ignorant; it was for this that Chekhov reproached Tolstoy. "Tolstoy's morality has ceased to affect me," he wrote. "At heart I don't approve of it. I myself have peasant blood, and no one can impress me with peasant virtues. I have believed in progress since my childhood. Sober reflection and a sense of justice tell me there is more love for mankind in electricity and steam than in chastity and fasting."

In short, he was a positivist—from modesty; a simple servant of enlightening truth who never for a moment claimed any of the liberties usually taken by the great. Once, when commenting on Bourget's *Disciple*, he inveighed vehemently against the disparagement of scientific materialism masquerading as idealism. "Such crusades are incomprehensible to me. To forbid a man the materialistic conception is to forbid him to seek the truth. Outside matter there is neither experience nor knowledge, and therefore no truth."

Chekhov's persistent self-doubts as an artist extended, if I am not mistaken, beyond his own self; they embraced art, above all literature. He found it repugnant to live alone "between my four walls"; he considered that the pursuit of art should always be complemented by practical, social activity in the world, among men, in the midst of life. Literature, to use his own words, was his mistress, while medicine was his lawful wife, toward whom he felt guilty of the infidelity committed with the other. Hence the harassing journey to Sakhalin, endangering his already precarious health, followed by his sensational report on the island's unspeakable conditions, a report that actually led to some reforms. Hence, too, his unremitting activity as a country doctor which went hand in hand with his literary work; the administration of the district hospital in Svenigorod near Moscow; the battle against cholera fought on his own small property in Melikhovo, where he succeeded in having isolation wards erected. It was here, too, that he acted as trustee to the village school. Meanwhile, his literary reputation continued to grow; but he eyed this growth with skepticism and a stricken conscience. "Am I not fooling the reader," he asked, "since I cannot answer the most important questions?"

These words had a profound effect upon me; it was thanks to them that I decided to delve deeper into Chekhov's life, one of the most moving and captivating biographies that I know. He came from Taganrog on the Sea of Azov in south Russia, a small provincial town where his father, a lower-middle-class bigot (whose own father had been a serf), kept a grocery store and bullied his wife and children. The old man also dabbled in ikon-painting, strummed amateurishly on the violin, had a passion for liturgical music, and organized a church choir in which his sons had to sing. These stray hobbies were probably responsible for the business going bankrupt while Anton Pavlovich was still at school, and for the father having to flee from his creditors to Moscow. Yet in the heart of this narrow, lower-middle-class bigot there evidently lurked some dim artistic seed, destined to germinate and unfold in only one of the offspring. True, one

of the elder brothers became a "publicist," the other a painter
—an insignificant publicist, and a painter who, like the former, drowned what talent he may have had in vodka: weak,
decrepit characters whom the only stable member of the
family tried in vain to support.

For the time being the boys had to help their father with
the selling of his wares, run errands, and on holidays get up
at three o'clock in the morning to rehearse with the choir for
the religious services. In addition there was the Taganrog
Latin school, a soul-destroying drill-ground in which both
teachers and pupils were instructed from above to stifle the
least sign of independent thought. Life was akin to hard labor, monotonous, vapid, oppressive. But one son, Anton, the
secretly chosen, had his own strange ways of compensating
for this dismal atmosphere. He possessed a natural bent for
gaiety and the poking of fun, for clowning and mimicry, a
talent which fed on observation and was translated into hi-
larious caricature. The boy could take off a simple-minded
deacon, a local official shaking his leg at a dance, a dentist,
a police sergeant's behavior in church. He could copy them
all so supremely well, in a manner so true to life, that the
whole school marveled. "Do that again!" they cried. "That's
really something! We saw it too, and it didn't seem funny.
But when this little devil does it, we burst out laughing. He
makes it seem more like life than life itself. This is something
new. Ha, ha, ha! What fun! Now then, enough of this irreverent horseplay! But listen, before you stop, do again the
police sergeant setting off to church! Just once more!"

What makes its appearance here is the primitive origin of
all art, the inclination to ape, the jester's desire and talent to
entertain, a gift that was to employ very different means in
the future, was to pour itself into very different forms; it
was to ally itself with spiritual principles, to undergo moral
ennoblement, and to rise from merely amusing trifles to soul-
stirring achievements. Yet even in his bitterest, most serious
moments Chekhov was never entirely to lose his sense of the

farcical, his work was always to retain much of the brilliant aping of the police sergeant and the dancing official. . . .

After the father had been obliged to close his shop and flee to Moscow, Anton Pavlovich, then sixteen, spent three more years in Taganrog to finish his education. For if his most cherished desire, to study medicine, were to be fulfilled, he had to graduate from Latin school. And graduate he did. Having passed through the three upper forms on a tiny scholarship supplemented by miserably paid lessons to younger students, he obtained his graduation certificate and followed his parents to Moscow, where he entered the university.

Did the young man who had escaped from the narrow, provincial existence feel happier in the great city? Did he breathe more freely? Alas, no one could breathe freely in Russia then. It was a stifling, gloomy life in which men, intimidated by brutal authority, slunk about in hypocritical submissiveness, censored, bullied, and bellowed at by the state. The country groaned under the ultra-autocratic regime of Alexander III and his ghastly minister Pobedonoszev —a regime of hopelessness. And among Chekhov's acquaintances many a fine mind, delicately balanced and gasping for the air of freedom, literally succumbed to hopelessness. Gleb Ouspenski, an honest portrayer of Russian peasant life, went out of his mind. Garshin, whose melancholic fiction Chekhov highly respected, committed suicide. The painter Levitan, with whom Anton Pavlovich was on friendly terms, also attempted to take his life. Vodka exerted an increasingly strong attraction among intellectuals. They drank from despair. Both of Chekhov's brothers drank, and rapidly came down in the world despite Anton's fervent pleadings to pull themselves together. They probably would have been drunkards had there been no Pobedonoszev, and they could, alas, have referred among others to dear, good Palmin the poet, another friend of Anton's, who also drank.

Anton Pavlovich did not take to drink, neither did he

grow melancholy or lose his mind. In the first place, he eagerly pursued the study of medicine, which was beyond the control of M. Pobedonoszev; as for the general despair, he armed himself against it as he had against the dreariness of Taganrog: he made fun, he caricatured the police sergeant, the stupid deacon, and the official at the ball. But he no longer took them off by mimicry, he aped them in writing. He sat in the noise and chaos of his parents' apartment, which he shared, and wrote for any comic paper that liked to indulge in a little cautious satire. He tossed off all kinds of odd things, very short, hastily jotted down: anecdotes, dialogues, humorous gossip, thumbnail sketches of provincial weddings, drunken tradesmen, bickering wives or those gone astray, an ex-sergeant who kept shouting at everybody—and all this with such zest that people would exclaim, just as they had at Taganrog: "This is really something! The knack he has! Do it again!"

And he did it again and again, exuberantly, inexhaustible in small observations and comical imitations of daily life, although to combine the exacting study of medicine with this public clowning must have put a considerable strain on the young man. For these sketches, after all, had to be shaped, given a point, something that required a mental effort, and considerable numbers of them had to be produced if the miserly fees were to accumulate sufficiently to pay not only for his studies but also to contribute substantially to the support of his parents, his younger brothers and sisters, for the father earned next to nothing and at nineteen Anton was the mainstay of the family. The name he used as provider for comic papers was Antosha Chekhonte. . . .

And then something strange occurred, something characteristic of the willful spirit of literature and proof of the unexpected consequences that can occur once this art is embarked upon at all, no matter how expedient, casual, or frivolous the reason may be. This spirit "knocks at the conscience"—as Antosha Chekhonte, the jester, said himself. He

has described in a letter how—amidst the comings and go-
ings in his parents' apartment, surrounded by screaming children, the sound of a music box and his father reading aloud
next door—he was sitting at an unprotected table, his literary
work before him *"knocking mercilessly at my conscience."*
This seemed hardly fair, considering the work was intended
merely as a joke to amuse the bourgeois world. But what a
moment ago I referred to as strange, characteristic, unexpected, is that gradually, without his knowledge or conscious
consent, there had crept into his sketches something originally not meant for them, something springing from the
conscience of literature as well as from his own personal conscience: something which, while still gay and entertaining,
contained a sad, bitter note, exposing and accusing life and
society, compassionate yet critical—in a word, literature. For
this note that had crept in was directly connected with writing itself, with form and language. This critical sadness, this
rebelliousness expresses the longing for a better reality, for a
purer, truer, nobler, more beautiful life, a worthier human
society. And this longing was reflected in the language, in
the obligation to treat it as a work of art, a "merciless" obligation that was undoubtedly part of the change that had
crept into Antosha's formless scribbling. Fifteen years were
to pass before Gorky pronounced judgment on this same Antosha: "As a stylist Chekhov has no equal, and future literary historians, reflecting on the development of the Russian
language, will maintain that this language has been created
by Pushkin, Turgenev, and Chekhov."

These words were uttered in 1900. Just now we are concerned with the years 1884-5. Having completed his studies,
Anton Pavlovich, then twenty-four, took a job as an intern
at the district hospital of Voskressensk, where he performed
autopsies on the corpses of suicides and others who had died
under suspicious circumstances. He continued, nevertheless,
to write comic sketches, for this had become a habit. Among
these stories a few slipped in—"The Death of an Official,"

"The Fat and the Lean," "A Delinquent"—whose composition had given him particular pleasure. Because their humor was tinged with bitterness, it is possible that they did not altogether please the general public, but they caused readers here and there to raise an eyebrow. One of these was D. W. Grigorovich. Who knows Dmitri Vasilievich Grigorovich? Not I. Frankly, I had never heard of him until I began to study Chekhov's life. And yet at that time he was a widely respected author, a distinguished man of letters who had earned a considerable reputation with his novels on the life of serfs. It was this famous, already elderly man, once a friend of Belinsky, later of Turgenev and Dostoevsky, who one day wrote a letter from St. Petersburg to the young Dr. Chekhov in Voskressensk near Moscow. It was a very serious letter, marking perhaps the most moving, surprising, and epoch-making event in Chekhov's life. "You possess, dear sir," he wrote, "a very exceptional talent which, I am convinced, has no need to recoil from the most difficult tasks. It would be a tragedy were you to squander your gifts on literary trifles. I feel the urge to implore you not to do this, but to concentrate on work of genuine artistic merit."

Anton Pavlovich read these lines in black and white, and under them the signature of the celebrated man. Probably never again in his life was he to feel so bewildered, so thrilled, so overwhelmed. "I almost broke into tears," he wrote in answer, "and feel that your letter has left a deep mark on my soul. I feel dazed and quite incapable of judging whether I deserve this high praise or not. . . . If I do possess a talent worthy of esteem, let me confess to the purity of your heart that I have not until now respected this gift of mine. . . . *There is always sufficient reason to be unfair to oneself, highly suspicious, and morbidly sensitive.* . . . Hitherto I have adopted an extremely frivolous, careless, and superficial attitude toward my literary activities. . . . I just wrote, taking care at all costs *not to waste on my stories those images and characters that are precious to me.* These, God knows why, I have protected and kept carefully hidden." This is what Chekhov wrote to the old Grigorovich in his letter of thanks which later became famous. Having written it, he went off to perform an autopsy or perhaps to visit a typhus case in the district hospital—let us say to a typhus case in memory of Lieutenant Klimov's spotted fever, the story of an illness written somewhat later with masterly skill from the patient's point of view by Anton Chekhov, who, after receiving that letter, never again signed himself Antosha Chekhonte.

Anton Pavlovich was granted but a short life. He was only twenty-nine when the first symptoms of tuberculosis appeared. As a doctor he recognized them for what they were and certainly harbored no illusions that his vitality could carry him to the patriarchal age of a Tolstoy. One wonders whether his awareness of his brief stay on earth did not largely contribute to his strange, skeptical, and infinitely endearing modesty, which continued to characterize his artistic and intellectual attitude, including even the instinct to make this modesty a special feature of his art, elevating it to a specific magic of his existence. Roughly twenty-five years —this was the time allowed him for the developing and perfecting of his creative talent, and he certainly made full use of the years. Some six hundred stories bear his name, not a few of which are "long short stories," among them masterpieces such as "Ward Number Six," in which a doctor, disgusted by the stupidity and misery of the world of normal men, forms such a close relationship with an interesting lunatic that this world declares him a lunatic, too, and locks him up. Although this eighty-seven-page story, written in 1892, avoids any direct accusation, it is so devastatingly symbolic of the corruption and hopelessness in Russia, of the degradation of mankind toward the end of the autocracy, that it prompted the young Lenin to say to his sister: "Last

night after finishing that story I felt very uneasy. I couldn't
sit still in my room. I had to get up and go out. I felt as
though I myself were locked up in Ward Number Six."

But while in the midst of quoting and praising I must certainly not forget to mention "A Tedious Tale," my favorite
among Chekhov's narrative works, a truly extraordinary,
fascinating story whose atmosphere of strange, gentle sadness
is unlike anything else in world literature. Not the least surprising feature of this overwhelming tale, announcing itself
as "tedious," is that it has been put into the mouth of an old
man by a man of thirty with infinite understanding. The old
man is a world-famous scholar, a general by rank, an Excellency, a term by which he frequently refers to himself in his
confessions. "My Excellency!" he says in a tone suggesting:
"Good Lord!" For, although high up in the official hierarchy, he has enough intelligence, self-criticism, and criticism
in general to look upon the fame and respect paid to him as
absurd. In the depths of his soul he is a desperate man because he realizes that, despite all its rewards, his life has always lacked a spiritual center, a "central idea," that basically
it has been a meaningless life. "Every feeling, every thought,"
he says, "lives isolated within me, and no analytical observer,
however experienced, could find in my judgments on science, the theater, literature, etc., etc., what is called a central
idea or the spirit of God in man. *And if this is lacking, then
there is nothing.* . . . It is therefore not at all surprising that
the last months of my life have been clouded by thoughts
and feelings worthy of a slave and a barbarian, and that now
I am indifferent to everything. If there is nothing in a human
being's life stronger and more important than outer circumstances, then indeed a common cold is sufficient to upset
his equilibrium, and all his pessimism as well as his great and
trivial thoughts have no more significance than symptoms—
nothing else. I am defeated. This being the case, there is no
point in continuing to think, no point in arguing. I shall just
sit and wait in silence for what is to come."

"And my ending is despair"—Prospero's last line keeps recurring to the mind while reading the confessions of the famous old Nikolai Stepanytsch. "Quite frankly," he says, "I
just don't like the popularity of my name. I feel it has de-
ceived me." When Anton Chekhov made the old man say
this and what has been quoted above, he was a young man.
Yet he had not long to live, and perhaps this was why he
managed to anticipate with such uncanny insight the mood
of old age. To the dying scholar he gave much of himself—
above all, this: "I just don't like the popularity of my name."
For Chekhov himself did not like his growing fame; "for
some reason [he] felt uneasy about it." Was he not deceiv-
ing his readers by dazzling them with his talent, since he
could not "answer the most important questions"? Why did
he write? What was his aim, his faith? Where was the "spirit
of God in man"? Where was the "central idea" of his life
and writing, "without which there is nothing"?

"A conscious life without a definite philosophy," he wrote
to a friend, "is no life, rather a burden and a nightmare."
Katya, a shipwrecked actress, the famous scholar's ward and
the only human being to whom he is still attached, for whom
he feels an aging man's secret tenderness, asks him out of profound confusion and despair: "What shall I do? Just one
word, Nikolai Stepanytsch, I implore you. What shall I do?"
And he is obliged to answer: "I don't know. Upon my honor
and conscience, Katya, I don't know." Whereupon she leaves
him.

The question "What's to be done?" keeps cropping up in a
deliberately confused manner throughout Chekhov's work;
the strange, helpless, stilted way in which his characters hold
forth on the problem of existence almost borders on the ludicrous. I can no longer remember in which story, but some-
where a lady appears and says: "Life should be observed as
through a prism—that's to say, it should be seen in refrac-
tions, should be divided into its simplest elements, and then
each element studied separately." His short stories and plays

seethe with this kind of dialogue. In part it may be just a satirical description of the Russian love for the interminable and fruitless philosophical discussion—a kind of persiflage that can also be found in other Russian writers. But in Chekhov's case it has a very special background, a specific, disconcertingly comical artistic function. For example, "My Life," a story told in the first person, is filled with arguments of this sort. The "I," with the nickname of "Better-than-Nothing," is a utopian socialist in revolt against the existing order; he believes in the necessity of manual labor for all, deserts his own, the educated class, and dedicates himself to a dismal, hard, ugly proletarian existence whose brutal reality exposes him to many painful disappointments. Sorrow over his son's eccentricity brings the father, a man devoted to tradition, to the grave, and it is also the young man's fault that his sister goes astray and comes to grief. One character, Doctor Blagovo, says to the narrator: "I respect you, you are a noble soul, a true idealist. But don't you think that if instead of spending all this will-power, intensity, and energy on changing your life you had spent it on gradually becoming, say, a great scientist or an artist, your life would have been both wider and deeper, in every respect more productive?" No, answers "Better-than-Nothing," what is of vital necessity is that the strong should not enslave the weak, the minority should not become a parasite of the majority; that everyone, the strong no less than the weak, the rich no less than the poor, should share equally in the struggle for existence, and in this respect there is no better means of leveling than manual labor and compulsory service for all. "But don't you think that if everyone, including the best men, the great philosophers and scientists, were to take part in the struggle for existence and spend their time breaking stones and painting roofs, it would mean a serious menace to progress?" This is a good question; but not good enough to prevent an even better or at least equally good answer. And from the subject of progress, the conversation moves on to its aims. Aims and limits of universal progress, in Doctor Blagovo's opinion, lie in infinity, and to contemplate progress as limited by man's needs and temporary theories he finds positively strange, to say the least.

What an argument! If the limits of progress lie in infinity, then its aims must be indefinite. *"How can man live without knowing what he is living for?"* "Granted. But this 'not knowing' is less boring than your 'knowing.' I am climbing a ladder which is called progress, civilization, culture. I keep on climbing higher and higher without knowing definitely where I am going, but for me this wonderful ladder alone makes life worth living. You, on the other hand, know what you are living for: you live so that some people should not enslave others, so that the painter and the man who grinds his paints for him should eat the same food. But surely this is the dull, humdrum, kitchen side of life! To live for that alone strikes me as nauseating. . . . We must keep in mind the great Unknown which awaits mankind in the distant future. . . ."

Blagovo is arguing with great fervor, yet it is clear that his mind is occupied with thoughts of another nature. "I suppose your sister is not coming?" he says, consulting his watch. "She mentioned yesterday that she might call on you this afternoon." So he has come simply to meet the sister with whom he is in love, has been talking just to while away the time! By this human motive underlying his words and clearly written in his face, anything he says turns to irony and is smilingly devalued. "Better-than-Nothing's" attempt radically to change his life is devalued, or at least rendered problematical by the degrading disappointments he encounters and the guilt he is taking upon himself in the process; the visitor's dialectic turns to irony by being used to kill time. The truth about life, to which the writer should be in duty bound, devalues his ideas and opinions. *This truth is by nature ironical*, and it can easily happen that a writer who puts the truth above everything else is reproached by the world with lack

of conviction, indifference to good and evil, lack of ideals
and ideas. Chekhov objected to reproaches of this kind. He
trusted the reader, he said, to fill in the suppressed "subjective"—that is, the critical—elements lacking in the story, to
supply for himself the ethical point of view. Why, then, his
"uneasiness," the dislike for his fame, this feeling of mis-
leading his readers with his talent because he could not answer the most important questions? What is the source of this
uncanny ability to put himself into the position of the despairing old man who realized that his life had lacked the
"central idea . . . without which there is nothing," and
who, to the bewildered girl's question: "What shall I do?"
was obliged to answer: "Upon my honor and conscience, I
don't know"?

If the truth about life is by nature ironical, then must not
art itself be by nature nihilistic? And yet art is so industrious!
Art is, so to speak, the very essence of work in its highest abstract form, the paradigm of all work, it is work itself, and for
its own sake. Chekhov believed in work as few others ever
have. Gorky said of him that he had "never known anyone feel so deeply that work is the basis of all culture as
Chekhov did." And indeed he worked incessantly, indefati-
gably, regardless of his delicate constitution and the debili-
tating nature of his disease, worked every day to the end.
What is more, he persisted in this heroic labor while con-
tinuously doubting its value, despite the guilty awareness
that it lacked the "central idea," that he had no answer to
the question "What can be done?" and that he was shirking
the issue by mere descriptions of life. "We just depict life as
it is," he said, "without taking one step further." Or: "As
things stand, the life of an artist has no point, and the more
talented he is, the stranger and more incomprehensible his
role becomes, because he is obviously working to amuse a
foul beast of prey, and by so doing helping to support the
existing order." By existing order is meant the unbearable
conditions under which Chekhov lived in the Russia of the

1890's. But his distress, his doubts about the value of his own work, his feeling for the strangeness and incomprehensibility of his role as an artist, such doubts are timeless and not confined to conditions prevailing in Russia at the end of the nineteenth century. By "conditions" is meant bad conditions, showing an unbridgeable gulf separating truth from reality, which always exists. Chekhov has fellow sufferers today, too, writers who do not feel at ease with their fame because they are "amusing a forlorn world without offering it a scrap of saving truth"—so we are told, at least—and who, like him, can identify themselves with the aged hero of "A Tedious Tale" who has no answer to the question "What shall I do?" These writers, too, are unable to say what the value of their own work is; nevertheless, they go on working, working to the end.

There must be something in this strange "nevertheless," it must have a meaning, and so give a meaning to work as well. Does work itself perhaps, however much it may look like amusement, contain something ethical, something of service to the human cause, leading in the end even to the "saving truth" toward which a bewildered world is stretching out its hands? Earlier in this essay I spoke of literature's spirit of willfulness, of its unexpected consequences, and tried to describe how this spirit, quite unintentionally on his part, entered the young Chekhov's scribblings, automatically raising their moral level. This process, continuing throughout his whole literary career, can be recognized at every phase. One biographer says of him: "What seems remarkable in Chekhov's development is the *close connection between his rise to the mastery of form* and the change in attitude toward his time. It was this attitude that determined his choice of subject matter, his characterization and control of action, and can be recognized in all of them. Indeed, here and there this new attitude is expressed through his protagonists as conscious reflection revealing an unerring instinct and a subtle power to distinguish between those forces which are soon to belong to the past and those of a new era pointing to the future." What I find interesting about this comment is the discovery of a connection between Chekhov's rise toward mastery of *form* and his growing sensitivity toward the social evils of his time —in other words, his deepening awareness of what is condemned by society and dying as well as of that which is to come; in short, the connection between the aesthetic and the ethical. It is surely this connection which gives to the industriousness of art its dignity, its meaning, its usefulness; it also explains Chekhov's immense respect for work itself, his disapproval of all idle parasitism, his increasingly outspoken condemnation of a life which, as he said, "is based on slavery."

This is a harsh verdict to pass on a bourgeois capitalist society proud of its humanitarianism and deaf to the notion of slavery. But our story-teller displayed a remarkably acute eye for the doubtfulness of human progress in general, and for the social and moral conditions following the liberation of the peasants in his native Russia—conditions which nevertheless do have a certain general validity. "Side by side with the gradual development of humane ideas," Chekhov made his "Better-than-Nothing" say, "the gradual growth of ideas of a very different order can be observed. Serfdom has been abolished, but [he could also have said: just because] capitalism is on the increase. Even now, in the very heyday of liberal ideas, the majority as usual has to feed, clothe, and defend the minority while itself remaining hungry, inadequately clothed, and defenseless. Such a state of affairs can easily be made to fit in with any ideological currents of thought you like, for *the art of enslaving is also gradually being refined*. We no longer flog our servants, but we practice slavery in more subtle ways; at least we know how to justify each particular case. Of course we hold humane ideals in high esteem, but if now, at the close of the nineteenth century, it were possible to shift the burden of our most unpleasant physiological functions onto the working class, we should certainly do so, and afterward justify ourselves by saying that if the best men, the great philosophers and scientists, were to waste their precious time on these functions, progress would seriously suffer."

This is but one sample of Chekhov's way of ridiculing the self-righteousness of the "progressivists." As a doctor he had a pronounced contempt for the palliatives with which these people treated the social sickness. He is extremely funny in the story "A Doctor's Visit," where he makes the governess of a wealthy manufacturer's family extol over sterlet and Madeira the blessings of these palliatives. "Our workers are very contented," she says. "Every winter in the factory we have theatrical performances in which the workers themselves take part. They also have lectures with a magic lantern, a splendid tea-room, and several other amenities. The workers are very devoted to us, and when they heard that my young lady had taken a turn for the worse, they ordered special prayers to be said. They may not be educated, but they do have feelings."

Yet the man from whose practice this story is told, head physician Korolyov, whose real name is Anton Chekhov, can only shake his head at her words. "While looking at the factory buildings and the barracks where the workers were asleep," we read, "he was reminded once more of what he always thought when he saw factories. Even though the men had theatrical performances, magic lanterns, factory doctors, and all manner of improvements, the workers he had met that day on his way from the station did not look in any way different from the men he had seen in his childhood before the existence of improvements and performances in factories. As a doctor with a sure judgment of chronic ailments whose prime cause was unknown and incurable, he also looked upon factories as an anomalous phenomenon whose cause could likewise be neither detected nor removed; and although he did not consider all improvements in the lives of factory hands to be superfluous, he nevertheless compared them with the patching up of incurable diseases." If cure at all, one can hear him say, then not the diseases, but their causes. "Infirmaries, schools, reading-rooms, and pharmacies are also nothing but tools of slavery under the given circumstances—that's my conviction." A conviction that must not allow us to forget that Chekhov himself founded schools and hospitals in his district. But this did not set his mind at rest. "What matters most," runs the sentence into which he increasingly condensed his thought, "is to break out of the rut; everything else is unimportant."

But, taking into account the all too "given" circumstances and the fact that everything has its incurable necessity, how was this to be done? What was the answer to the question: "What can we do?" The uneasiness caused by this question haunts numerous characters in Chekhov's stories. In "A Doctor's Visit" he coined the phrase "honorable sleeplessness." In this story Doctor Korolyov has been summoned to the intelligent, unhappy young lady, heiress to a million rubles and some factories, because she suffers from nervous fits and insomnia. "It's not that I feel ill," she says herself, "I am just uneasy and filled with anxiety, because it has to be like this and cannot be otherwise." It is quite clear to the doctor what he ought to tell her: Give up the five factories and the million as soon as possible and cast that devil out! And it is equally clear to him that she thinks the same, but is simply waiting to have it confirmed by someone she trusts. But how can he put it to her? One shrinks from asking a condemned man why he has been condemned, and it is also painful to ask the wealthy why they need so much money, why they make such poor use of their wealth, why they don't give it away, even when they realize it is the cause of their unhappiness. And once this kind of conversation is begun it invariably becomes embarrassing, painful, and boring. This is why he answers her frankly but in a consolatory tone: "It's in your role as factory-owner and wealthy heiress that you are dissatisfied; you don't feel entitled to wealth, so you cannot sleep. This is

preferable, of course, to your being satisfied, to sleeping well
and believing that all is as it should be. *You are suffering from
an honorable sleeplessness.* Whatever else it may be, this is a
good sign. The notion that our parents could have had a conversation like this is unthinkable; they did not discuss things
at night, they slept soundly. But we of our generation sleep
badly, torment ourselves, talk a great deal, and are all the
time trying to decide whether we are right or not. For our
children and grandchildren this question of being in the right
or not will already have been decided. They will have a
clearer vision. Fifty years from now life will be beautiful. . . ."

Will it? One has to face the fact that man is a failure. His
conscience, which belongs to the spirit, will probably never
be brought into harmony with his nature, his reality, his social condition, and there will always be "honorable sleeplessness" for those who for some unfathomable reason feel
responsible for human fate and life. If anyone ever suffered
from this, it was Chekhov the artist. All his work was honorable sleeplessness, a search for the right, redeeming word in
answer to the question: "What are we to do?" The word
was difficult, if not impossible, to find. The only thing he
knew for certain was that idleness is the worst, that man has
to work because idleness means letting others work for him,
means exploitation and oppression. In his last story, "Betrothed," Sasha—who, like Chekhov, is consumptive and soon
to die—says to Nadya, another girl unable to sleep: "Please
understand that if your mother and grandmother do nothing, it means that others are working for them, that they are
usurping someone else's life. Do you think this is decent?
Isn't there something wrong? . . . Dear, sweet Nadya, go
away! Show them that you are sick of this stagnant, gray,
sinful life! Prove it to yourself! I swear you won't regret it.
You will go away; you will study and let yourself be guided
by your fate. As soon as you have taken your life into your
own hands, everything will be different. What matters most

is to break out of the rut; everything else is unimportant. Now, shall we leave tomorrow?" And Nadya really does go. She leaves her family, her ineffectual fiancé, renounces marriage, and escapes. It is a flight from the shackles of class, from a way of life felt to be out of date, false, and "sinful," which keeps recurring in Chekhov's work, the same flight on which the aged Tolstoy embarked at the last moment.

Some time later when Nadya, the escaped bride, pays a visit to her old home, it seems to her "that everything in the town had grown old and out of date, and was just waiting either for the end or for the beginning of a bright, new life." Sooner or later this new life was bound to come. "The time will come when not a trace will remain of Grandmother's house, where things were arranged in such a way that the four servants had to live in one room in the basement, in filth—one day all this will be forgotten, no one will even remember the house." Indeed, poor Sasha himself has told her: "Not a stone of your town will be left standing, everything will be blown up from its foundations, everything will be changed as though by magic, and huge, magnificent houses . . . with beautiful gardens and fountains will stand here, a new kind of people will live here, and every man will know what he is living for. . . ." This is one of the euphoric visions of the future which Chekhov, who in his heart knew that "life is an insoluble problem," occasionally permitted either himself or one of his characters. These visions have a somewhat feverish quality, suggesting the tender reveries of a consumptive, as when he speaks of the "perhaps imminent day when life will be as bright and joyful as a peaceful Sunday morning." The outlines of his vision of human perfection in the future are vague. It is the picture of a union between beauty and truth based on work. But in his dream of the "huge, magnificent houses . . . with beautiful gardens and fountains" that are to rise in place of the dying, outdated town, is there not something of the socialist passion for building with which modern Russia, despite all the horror and the hostility it provokes, impresses the Western world?

Chekhov had no contact whatever with the working class, nor had he studied Marx. Although he wrote about work, he was not, like Gorky, a workers' poet. Yet he expressed his grief over social injustice in sounds that moved the hearts of his people, as in that tragic, magnificent social panorama "Peasants." Here at a religious festival the ikon of the Holy Virgin, "The Giver of Life," is carried round from village to village in a procession. In the midst of the dust and noise a vast crowd of villagers and strangers surges forward to meet the ikon; the people stretch out their hands to it, gaze at it eagerly, weeping: "Patroness! Mother!" "It was as though everyone suddenly realized that there was no void between heaven and earth, that the rich and powerful had not taken possession of everything, that there still existed a refuge from injury, from slavish bondage, from crushing unendurable poverty, from the terrible vodka. . . . Patroness! Mother! But hardly had the thanksgiving service ended and the ikon been carried off, when everything went on in the same old way, and the sounds of coarse drunken voices could be heard again from the tavern."

The compassion and bitterness about everything going on as before is authentic Chekhov, and I would not be surprised if this author's popularity, so spontaneously manifested at his death and funeral in Moscow, were based on such descriptions. This demonstration caused a government newspaper to remark that Anton Pavlovich had probably belonged to the "stormy petrels of the Revolution."

He did not look like a stormy petrel, nor like the moujik-turned-genius Tolstoy, nor like Nietzsche's pale criminal. The photographs show a slender man dressed in the fashion prevailing at the end of the nineteenth century: a starched collar, a pince-nez on a ribbon, short goatee, regular features marked by suffering and friendly melancholy. These features suggest intelligent attention, unassumingness, skepticism, and kindness. It is the face, the deportment of a man who does not make much fuss about himself. And if he already looked upon Tolstoy's teaching as "despotic" and described Dostoevsky's work as "good, but immodest, pretentious," it is easy to imagine how grotesque the arrogance of an empty mind must have appeared to him. Whenever he portrays this type, he is extremely funny. Many decades ago I saw his play *Uncle Vanya* performed in Munich. It is one of his quiet, light-stepping plays that spring entirely from the feeling for a dying, outdated, all but fictitious existence, the world of the landowning class; a play that replaces all dramatic, spectacular effects by the most subtle intensity of lyrical mood—a mood of end and farewell. In it appears a senile celebrity, a caricature of the hero of "A Tedious Tale," an emeritus professor and privy councillor who writes about art without the slightest knowledge of the subject, and who, moreover, tyrannizes the whole house with his sniveling old-age self-pity, his imagined importance, and his gout: a nonentity convinced of his dignity. It is to him that a lady says when kissing him good-by: "*Do get yourself photographed again,* Alexander Vladimirovich!" Throughout my life whenever I've thought of: "Do get yourself photographed again, Alexander Vladimirovich!" I've had to laugh. And when I sometimes feel like saying to this person or that: "Get yourself photographed!" it is Chekhov's doing.

As for him, he did let himself be photographed—when he had to. The portraits do not betray any signs of a tempestuous emotional life; it is as though this man had been too modest even for passion. The story of his life mentions no great infatuation for a woman, and his biographers believe that he, who wrote so brilliantly about love, never experienced erotic ecstasy. In the country at Melikhovo a beautiful, impulsive girl called Lydia Mesinova was a frequent guest; she fell desperately in love with him, and he went so far as to exchange letters with her. But his *lettres d'amour* are said to have been written in an ironical vein and to show a reluctance to express any deep emotion, a result perhaps of his illness. The pretty Lydia herself admitted that he twice turned her down, whereupon she consoled herself with the writer Potapenko, another visitor to Melikhovo and, incidentally, a married man. But if Lydia could make nothing of Chekhov, he knew what to make of the episode, which he wove into his most frequently produced play, *The Seagull.*

Only three years before his death, however, he did marry; a marriage that took place thanks to his happy relationship with the Moscow Art Theatre and his friendship with Stanislavsky, for his bride was the talented actress Olga Knipper. Letters to her in his own hand have survived, and they, too, are most reticent and confined to a playful, ironical tone.

Owing to his marriage, his friendship with Gorky, and his cordial relations with Tolstoy, who spent some time convalescing in a castle near Yalta, these last years in the Crimea, where his consumption obliged him to live, were perhaps the happiest of Chekhov's life. It was also at Yalta that he was visited by the whole cast of the Moscow Art Theatre, which had come there in order to act his plays before him. His election to honorary membership in the literary section of the St. Petersburg Academy of Science gave the sick man a childish pleasure. But two years later, when Gorky's election was annulled on account of his radical opinions, Chekhov, like Korolenko, resigned in protest.

His last story was "Betrothed" (1903), his last play *The Cherry Orchard.* In both works a spirit, facing dissolution with composure and making no fuss even about illness and death, sowed a seed of hope on the very brink of the grave. His life's work, although it laid no claim to the monumental proportions of the epic, nevertheless encompassed the whole of Russia, that vast country's natural landscape forming the background to the appallingly unnatural conditions of its pre-revolutionary era. "The impudence and idleness of the strong, the ignorance and animal submission of the weak, everywhere unbelievable poverty, oppression, degeneracy, alcoholism, hypocrisy, and dishonesty . . ." Yet the nearer his end approached, the more movingly an inner light of faith in the future flowed round the dark picture, the more fervently the poet's loving eye looked forward to a coming community of human beings, proud, free, and active, to "a new, dignified, and sensible way of life on whose threshold we may already be standing, of whose appearance we occasionally get a glimpse."

"Good-by, my dear, dear Sasha," says Nadya, the "Betrothed," to the dead man who has persuaded her to flee from a false existence. "And before her mind there rose a vision of a new life, wide and free, and this new life, still obscure and full of mystery, called to her and beckoned her." A dying man wrote those lines shortly before his end—and perhaps it was nothing but the mystery of death that was calling and beckoning. Or may we believe that the passionate longing of a poet can actually alter life?

Let me admit that I have written these pages with deep sympathy, stirred by the poetry of my theme. Chekhov's ironical attitude toward fame, the doubts he felt concerning the sense and value of his work, his disbelief in his own greatness contain in themselves the elements of a quiet, modest greatness. "Dissatisfaction with oneself," he said, "is one of the foundation stones of every real talent." Here his very modesty becomes self-affirmative. Rejoice in your dissatisfaction, he is implying, for it proves that you are more worthy than the self-satisfied—possibly even great. None of which diminishes the sincerity of his doubt and self-dissatisfaction. For him work, pursued relentlessly to the end with the awareness that one has no answers to the final questions, while one's conscience pricks one for throwing dust in the eye of the reader, remains a strange obligation in spite of all. It comes to this: One "entertains a forlorn world by telling stories without ever being able to offer it the trace of a saving truth." To poor Katya's question: "What am I to do?"

one can but answer: "Upon my honor and conscience, I don't know." Nevertheless, one goes on working, telling stories, giving form to truth, hoping darkly, sometimes almost confidently, that truth and serene form will avail to set free the human spirit and prepare mankind for a better, lovelier, worthier life.

Translated by Tania and James Stern

APPENDIX

A WEARY HOUR

(1905)

HE got up from the table, his little, fragile writing-desk; got up as though desperate, and with hanging head crossed the room to the tall, thin, pillar-like stove in the opposite corner. He put his hands to it; but the hour was long past midnight and the tiles were nearly stone cold. Not getting even this little comfort that he sought, he leaned his back against them and, coughing, drew together the folds of his dressing-gown, between which a draggled lace shirt-frill stuck out; he snuffed hard through his nostrils to get a little air, for as usual he had a cold.

It was a particular, a sinister cold, which scarcely ever quite disappeared. It inflamed his eyelids and made the flanges of his nose all raw; in his head and limbs it lay like a heavy, somber intoxication. Or was this cursed confinement to his room, to which the doctor had weeks ago condemned him, to blame for all his languor and flabbiness? God knew if it was the right thing—perhaps so, on account of his chronic catarrh and the spasms in his chest and belly. And for weeks on end now, yes, weeks, bad weather had reigned in Jena—hateful, horrible weather, which he felt in every nerve of his body—cold, wild, gloomy. The December wind roared in the stove-pipe with a desolate godforsaken sound—he might have been wandering on a heath, by night and storm, his soul full of unappeasable grief. Yet this close confinement—that was not good either; not good for thought, nor for the rhythm of the blood, where thought was engendered.

The six-sided room was bare and colorless and devoid of cheer: a whitewashed ceiling wreathed in tobacco smoke, walls covered with trellis-patterned paper and hung with silhouettes in oval frames, half a dozen slender-legged pieces of furniture; the whole lighted by two candles burning at the head of the manuscript on the writing-table. Red curtains draped the upper part of the window-frames; mere festooned wisps of cotton they were, but red, a warm, sonorous red, and he loved them and would not have parted from them; they gave a little air of ease and charm to the bald unlovely poverty of his surroundings. He stood by the stove and blinked repeatedly, straining his eyes across at the work from which he had just fled: that load, that weight, that gnawing conscience, that sea which to drink up, that frightful task which to perform, was all his pride and all his misery, at once his heaven and his hell. It dragged, it stuck, it would not budge—and now again . . . ! It must be the weather; or his catarrh, or his fatigue. Or was it the work? Was the thing itself an unfortunate conception, doomed from its beginning to despair?

He had risen in order to put a little space between him and his task, for physical distance would often result in improved perspective, a wider view of his material and a better chance of conspectus. Yes, the mere feeling of relief on turning away from the battlefield had been known to work like an inspiration. And a more innocent one than that purveyed by alcohol or strong, black coffee.

The little cup stood on the side-table. Perhaps it would help him out of the impasse? No, no, not again! Not the doctor only, but somebody else too, a more important somebody, had cautioned him against that sort of thing—another person, who lived over in Weimar and for whom he felt a love which was a mixture of hostility and yearning. That was a wise man. He knew how to live and create; did not abuse himself; was full of self-regard.

Quiet reigned in the house. There was only the wind, driving down the Schlossgasse and dashing the rain in gusts against the panes. They were all asleep—the landlord and his family, Lotte and the children. And here he stood by the cold stove, awake, alone, tormented; blinking across at the work in which his morbid self-dissatisfaction would not let him believe.

His neck rose long and white out of his stock, and his knock-kneed legs showed between the skirts of his dressing-gown. The red hair was smoothed back from a thin, high forehead; it retreated in bays from his veined white temples and hung down in thin locks over the ears. His nose was aquiline, with an abrupt whitish tip; above it the well-marked line of the brows almost met. They were darker than his hair and gave the deep-set, inflamed eyes a tragic, staring look. He could not breathe through his nose; so he opened his thin lips and made the freckled, sickly cheeks look even more sunken thereby.

No, it was a failure, it was all hopelessly wrong. The army ought to have been brought in! The army was the root of the whole thing. But it was impossible to present it before the eyes of the audience—and was art powerful enough thus to enforce the imagination? Besides, his hero was no hero; he was contemptible, he was frigid. The situation was wrong, the language was wrong; it was a dry pedestrian lecture, good for a history class, but as drama absolutely hopeless!

Very good, then, it was over. A defeat. A failure. Bankruptcy. He would write to Körner, the good Körner, who believed in him, who clung with childlike faith to his genius. He would scoff, scold, beseech—this friend of his; would remind him of the *Don Carlos*, which likewise had issued out of doubts and pains and rewritings and after all the anguish turned out to be something really fine, a genuine masterpiece. But times were changed. Then he had been a man still capable of taking a strong, confident grip on a thing and giving it triumphant shape. Doubts and struggles? Yes. And ill he had been, perhaps more ill than now; a fugitive, oppressed and hungry, at odds with the world; humanly speaking, a beggar. But young, still young! Each time, however low he had sunk, his resilient spirit had leaped up anew; upon the hour of affliction had followed the feeling of triumphant self-confidence. That came no more, or hardly ever, now. There might be one night of glowing exaltation—when the fires of his genius lighted up an impassioned vision of all that he might do if only they burned on; but it had always to be paid for with a week of enervation and gloom. Faith in the future, his guiding star in times of stress, was dead. Here was the despairing truth: the years of need and nothingness, which he had thought of as the painful testing-time, turned out to have been the rich and fruitful ones; and now that a little happiness had fallen to his lot, now that he had ceased to be an intellectual freebooter and occupied a position of civic dignity, with office and honors, wife and children—now he was exhausted, worn out. To give up, to own himself beaten—that was all there was left to do. He groaned; he pressed his hands to his eyes and dashed up and down the room like one possessed. What he had just thought was

so frightful that he could not stand still on the spot where he had
thought it. He sat down on a chair by the further wall and stared
gloomily at the floor, his clasped hands hanging down between
his knees.

His conscience . . . how loudly his conscience cried out! He
had sinned, sinned against himself all these years, against the delicate instrument that was his body. Those youthful excesses, the
nights without sleep, the days spent in close, smoke-laden air,
straining his mind and heedless of his body; the narcotics with
which he had spurred himself on—all that was now taking its
revenge.

And if it did—then he would defy the gods, who decreed the
guilt and then imposed the penalties. He had lived as he had to
live, he had not had time to be wise, not time to be careful. Here
in this place in his chest, when he breathed, coughed, yawned,
always in the same spot came this pain, this piercing, stabbing,
diabolical little warning; it never left him, since that time in
Erfurt five years ago when he had catarrhal fever and inflamma-
tion of the lungs. What was it warning him of? Ah, he knew
only too well what it meant—no matter how the doctor chose to
put him off. He had no time to be wise and spare himself, no
time to save his strength by submission to moral laws. What he
wanted to do he must do soon, do quickly, do today.

And the moral laws? . . . Why was it that precisely sin, surrender to the harmful and the consuming, actually seemed to him
more moral than any amount of wisdom and frigid self-
discipline? Not that constituted morality: not the contemptible
knack of keeping a good conscience—rather the struggle and
compulsion, the passion and pain.

Pain . . . how his breast swelled at the word! He drew himself up and folded his arms; his gaze, beneath the close-set auburn
brows, was kindled by the nobility of his suffering. No man was
utterly wretched so long as he could still speak of his misery in
high-sounding and noble words. One thing only was indispensable; the courage to call his life by large and fine names. Not to
ascribe his sufferings to bad air and constipation; to be well
enough to cherish emotions, to scorn and ignore the material.
Just on this one point to be naïve, though in all else sophisticated.
To believe, to have strength to believe, in suffering. . . . But he
did believe in it; so profoundly, so ardently, that nothing which
came to pass with suffering could seem to him either useless or
evil. His glance sought the manuscript, and his arms tightened

across his chest. Talent itself—was that not suffering? And if the manuscript over there, his unhappy effort, made him suffer, was not that quite as it should be—a good sign, so to speak? His talents had never been of the copious, ebullient sort; were they to become so, he would feel mistrustful. That only happened with beginners and bunglers, with the ignorant and easily satisfied, whose life was not shaped and disciplined by the possession of a gift. For a gift, my friends down there in the audience, a gift is not anything simple, not anything to play with; it is not mere ability. At bottom it is a compulsion; a critical knowledge of the ideal, a permanent dissatisfaction, which rises only through suffering to the height of its powers. And it is to the greatest, the most unsatisfied, that their gift is the sharpest scourge. Not to complain, not to boast; to think modestly, patiently of one's pain; and if not a day in the week, not even an hour, be free from it— what then? To make light and little of it all, of suffering and achievement alike—that was what made a man great.

He stood up, pulled out his snuff-box and sniffed eagerly, then suddenly clasped his hands behind his back and strode so briskly through the room that the flames of the candles flickered in the draft. Greatness, distinction, world conquest, and an imperishable name! To be happy and unknown, what was that by comparison? To be known—known and loved by all the world—ah, they might call that egotism, those who knew nought of the urge, nought of the sweetness of this dream! Everything out of the ordinary is egotistic, in proportion to its suffering. "Speak for yourselves," it says, "ye without mission on this earth, ye whose life is so much easier than mine!" And Ambition says: "Shall my sufferings be vain? No, they must make me great!"

The nostrils of his great nose dilated, his gaze darted fiercely about the room. His right hand was thrust hard and far into the opening of his dressing-gown, his left arm hung down, the fist clenched. A fugitive red played in the gaunt cheeks—a glow thrown up from the fire of his artistic egoism: that passion for his own ego, which burned unquenchably in his being's depths. Well he knew it, the secret intoxication of this love! Sometimes he needed only to contemplate his own hand, to be filled with the liveliest tenderness toward himself, in whose service he was bent on spending all the talent, all the art that he owned. And he was right so to do, there was nothing base about it. For deeper still than his egoism lay the knowledge that he was freely consuming and sacrificing himself in the service of a high ideal, not as a virtue, of course, but rather out of sheer necessity. And this was his ambition: that no one should be greater than he who had not also suffered more for the sake of the high ideal. No one. He stood still, his hand over his eyes, his body turned aside in a posture of shrinking and avoidance. For already the inevitable thought had stabbed him: the thought of that other man, that radiant being, so sense-endowed, so divinely unconscious, that man over there in Weimar, whom he loved and hated. And once more, as always, in deep disquiet, in feverish haste, there began working within him the inevitable sequence of his thoughts: he must assert and define his own nature, his own art, against that other's. Was that other greater? Wherein, then, and why? If he won, would he have sweated blood to do so? If he lost, would his downfall be a tragic sight? He was no hero, no; a god, perhaps. But it was easier to be a god than a hero. Yes, things were easier for him. He was wise, he was deft, he knew how to distinguish between knowing and creating; perhaps that was why he was so blithe and carefree, such an effortless and gushing spring! But if creation was divine, knowledge was heroic, and he who created in knowledge was hero as well as god.

The will to face difficulties . . . Did anyone realize what discipline and self-control it cost him to shape a sentence or follow out a hard train of thought? For, after all, he was ignorant, undisciplined, a slow, dreamy enthusiast. One of Caesar's letters was harder to write than the most effective scene—and was it not almost for that very reason higher? From the first rhythmical urge of the inward creative force toward matter, toward the material, toward casting in shape and form—from that to the thought, the image, the word, the line—what a struggle, what a Gethsemane! Everything that he wrote was a marvel of yearning after form, shape, line, body; of yearning after the sunlit world of that other man who had only to open his godlike lips and straightway call the bright unshadowed things he saw by name!

And yet—and despite that other man. Where was there an artist, a poet, like himself? Who like him created out of nothing, out of his own breast? A poem was born as music in his soul, as pure, primitive essence, long before it put on a garment of metaphor from the visible world. History, philosophy, passion were no more than pretexts and vehicles for something which had little to do with them, but was at home in orphic depths. Words and conceptions were keys upon which his art played and made vibrate the hidden strings. No one realized. The good souls praised him, indeed, for the power of feeling with which he struck one note or another. And his favorite note, his final emotional appeal, the great bell upon which he sounded his summons to the highest feasts of the soul—many there were who responded to its sound. Freedom! But in all their exaltation, certainly he meant by the word both more and less than they did. Freedom— what was it? A self-respecting middle-class attitude toward thrones and princes? Surely not that. When one thinks of all that the spirit of man has dared to put into the word! Freedom from what? After all, from what? Perhaps, indeed, even from happiness, from human happiness, that silken bond, that tender, sacred tie. . . .

From happiness. His lips quivered. It was as though his glance turned inward upon himself; slowly his face sank into his hands. . . . He stood by the bed in the next room, where the flowered curtains hung in motionless folds across the window, and the lamp shed a bluish light. He bent over the sweet head on the pillow . . . a ringlet of dark hair lay across her cheek, that had the paleness of pearl; the childlike lips were open in slumber. "My wife! Beloved, did you yield to my yearning and come to me to be my joy? And that you are. . . . Lie still and sleep; nay, lift not those sweet shadowy lashes and gaze up at me, as sometimes with your great, dark, questioning, searching eyes. I love you so! By God I swear it. It is only that sometimes I am tired out, struggling at my self-imposed task, and my feelings will not respond. And I must not be too utterly yours, never utterly happy in you, for the sake of my mission."

He kissed her, drew away from her pleasant, slumbrous warmth, looked about him, turned back to the outer room. The clock struck; it warned him that the night was already far spent; but likewise it seemed to be mildly marking the end of a weary hour. He drew a deep breath, his lips closed firmly; he went back and took up his pen. No, he must not brood, he was too far down for that. He must not descend into chaos; or at least he must not stop there. Rather out of chaos, which is fullness, he must draw up to the light whatever he found there fit and ripe for form. No brooding! Work! Define, eliminate, fashion, complete!

And complete it he did, that effort of a laboring hour. He brought it to an end, perhaps not to a good end, but in any case to an end. And being once finished, lo, it was also good. And

from his soul, from music and idea, new works struggled upward
to birth and, taking shape, gave out light and sound, ringing and
shimmering, and giving hint of their infinite origin—as in a shell
we hear the sighing of the sea whence it came.

Translated by H. T. Lowe-Porter

The Principal Works of Thomas Mann

First Editions in German

DER KLEINE HERR FRIEDEMANN
[Little Herr Friedemann]. Tales
Berlin, S. Fischer Verlag. 1898

BUDDENBROOKS
Novel *Berlin, S. Fischer Verlag.* 1901

TRISTAN
Contains *Tonio Kröger*. Tales *Berlin, S. Fischer Verlag.* 1903

FIORENZA
Drama *Berlin, S. Fischer Verlag.* 1905

KÖNIGLICHE HOHEIT
[Royal Highness]. Novel *Berlin, S. Fischer Verlag.* 1909

DER TOD IN VENEDIG
[Death in Venice]. Short novel *Berlin, S. Fischer Verlag.* 1913

DAS WUNDERKIND
[The Infant Prodigy]. Tales *Berlin, S. Fischer Verlag.* 1914

BETRACHTUNGEN EINES UNPOLITISCHEN
Autobiographical reflections *Berlin, S. Fischer Verlag.* 1918

HERR UND HUND
[A Man and His Dog]. Idyll
Contains also *Gesang vom Kindchen,* an idyll in verse
Berlin, S. Fischer Verlag. 1919

WÄLSUNGENBLUT
Tale *München, Phantasus Verlag.* 1921

BEKENNTNISSE DES HOCHSTAPLERS FELIX KRULL
Fragment of a novel *Stuttgart, Deutsche Verlags-Anstalt.*

BEMÜHUNGEN
Essays *Berlin, S. Fischer Verlag.* 1922

REDE UND ANTWORT
Essays *Berlin, S. Fischer Verlag.* 1922

DER ZAUBERBERG
[The Magic Mountain]. Novel *Berlin, S. Fischer Verlag.* 1924

THE PRINCIPAL WORKS OF THOMAS MANN

UNORDNUNG UND FRÜHES LEID
[Disorder and Early Sorrow]. Short novel
KINO   *Berlin, S. Fischer Verlag.*   1926
  Fragment of a novel   *Berlin, S. Fischer Verlag.*   1926

PARISER RECHENSCHAFT
  Travelogue   *Berlin, S. Fischer Verlag.*   1926

DEUTSCHE ANSPRACHE
  Ein Appell an die Vernunft *Berlin, S. Fischer Verlag.*   1930

DIE FORDERUNG DES TAGES
  Essays   *Berlin, S. Fischer Verlag.*   1930

MARIO UND DER ZAUBERER
[Mario and the Magician]. Short novel
                            Berlin, S. Fischer Verlag.   1930

GOETHE ALS REPRÄSENTANT DES
    BÜRGERLICHEN ZEITALTERS
  Lecture   *Berlin, S. Fischer Verlag.*   1932

JOSEPH UND SEINE BRÜDER
[Joseph and His Brothers]. Novel
  I. Die Geschichten Jaakobs. 1933.
  II. Der junge Joseph. 1934.
  III. Joseph in Ägypten. 1936.
  IV. Joseph, der Ernährer. 1943.
                  I, II, Berlin, S. Fischer Verlag.
                  III, Vienna, Bermann-Fischer Verlag.
                  IV, Stockholm, Bermann-Fischer Verlag.

LEIDEN UND GRÖSSE DER MEISTER
  Essays   *Berlin, S. Fischer Verlag.*   1935

FREUD UND DIE ZUKUNFT
  Lecture   *Vienna, Bermann-Fischer Verlag.*   1936

EIN BRIEFWECHSEL
[An Exchange of Letters]
                  Zürich, Dr. Oprecht & Helbling AG.   1937

DAS PROBLEM DER FREIHEIT
  Essay   *Stockholm, Bermann-Fischer Verlag.*

SCHOPENHAUER
  Essay   *Stockholm, Bermann-Fischer Verlag.*

ACHTUNG, EUROPA!
  Manifesto   *Stockholm, Bermann-Fischer Verlag.*

DIE SCHÖNSTEN ERZÄHLUNGEN
Contains *Tonio Kröger, Der Tod in Venedig, Unordnung und frühes Leid, Mario und der Zauberer*
Stockholm, Bermann-Fischer Verlag. 1938

LOTTE IN WEIMAR
[The Beloved Returns]. Novel
Stockholm, Bermann-Fischer Verlag. 1939

DIE VERTAUSCHTEN KÖPFE
Eine indische Legende [The Transposed Heads]
Stockholm, Bermann-Fischer Verlag. 1940

DEUTSCHE HÖRER
[Listen, Germany!] Broadcasts
Stockholm, Bermann-Fischer Verlag. 1942

DAS GESETZ
[The Tables of the Law]
Stockholm, Bermann-Fischer Verlag. 1944

DOKTOR FAUSTUS: DAS LEBEN DES DEUTSCHEN TONSETZERS ADRIAN LEVERKÜHN, ERZÄHLT VON EINEM FREUNDE
Novel   Stockholm, Bermann-Fischer Verlag. 1947

DER ERWÄHLTE
[The Holy Sinner]. Novel
Frankfurt am Main, S. Fischer Verlag. 1951

DIE BETROGENE
[The Black Swan]. Short Novel
Frankfurt am Main, S. Fischer Verlag. 1953

ALTES UND NEUES: Kleine Prosa aus fünf Jahrzehnten. [Small prose pieces of five decades]
Frankfurt am Main, S. Fischer Verlag. 1953

BEKENNTNISSE DES HOCHSTAPLERS FELIX KRULL: DER MEMOIREN ERSTER TEIL [Confessions of Felix Krull]. Novel
Frankfurt am Main, S. Fischer Verlag. 1954

NACHLESE: Prosa 1951–1955
Frankfurt am Main, S. Fischer Verlag. 1956

American Editions in Translation

published by ALFRED A. KNOPF, *New York*

ROYAL HIGHNESS: A NOVEL OF GERMAN COURT LIFE
Translated by A. Cecil Curtis   1916

BUDDENBROOKS
Translated by H. T. Lowe-Porter   1924

DEATH IN VENICE AND OTHER STORIES
Translated by Kenneth Burke. Contains Der Tod in
Venedig, Tristan, *and* Tonio Kröger (*out of print*)*   1925

THE MAGIC MOUNTAIN
Translated by H. T. Lowe-Porter. Two volumes   1927

CHILDREN AND FOOLS
*Translated by Herman George Scheffauer. Nine stories,
including translations of* Der kleine Herr Friedemann
and Unordnung and frühes Leid (*out of print*)*   1928

THREE ESSAYS
*Translated by H. T. Lowe-Porter. Contains translations
of* Friedrich und die grosse Koalition *from* Rede und
Antwort, *and of* Goethe und Tolstoi *and* Okkulte
Erlebnisse *from* Bemühungen   1929

EARLY SORROW
Translated by Herman George Scheffauor (*out of print*)*   1930

A MAN AND HIS DOG
Translated by Herman George Scheffauer (*out of print*)*   1930

DEATH IN VENICE
*A new translation by H. T. Lowe-Porter, with an Intro-
duction by Ludwig Lewisohn.*   1930

MARIO AND THE MAGICIAN
Translated by H. T. Lowe-Porter (*out of print*)*   1931

PAST MASTERS AND OTHER PAPERS
Translated by H. T. Lowe-Porter (*out of print*)   1933

JOSEPH AND HIS BROTHERS
I. Joseph and His Brothers (The Tales of Jacob)   1934
II. Young Joseph   1935
III. Joseph in Egypt   1938
IV. Joseph the Provider   1944
The complete work in 1 volume   1948
Translated by H. T. Lowe-Porter

STORIES OF THREE DECADES
*Translated by H. T. Lowe-Porter. Contains all of Thomas
Mann's fiction prior to 1940 except the long novels*   1936

AN EXCHANGE OF LETTERS
Translated by H. T. Lowe-Porter †   1937

---

* Included in *Stories of Three Decades,* translated by H. T. Lowe-
Porter.
† Also included in *Order of the Day.*

† Also included in *Order of the Day.*

A NOTE ABOUT THE AUTHOR

THOMAS MANN was born in 1875 in the ancient Hanseatic town of Lübeck, of a line of influential merchants. His father had been a senator and the mayor of the Free City; his mother was of German-Creole descent.

Mann was anything but a brilliant student at the local *Gymnasium*. He was nineteen when he moved to Munich and took a job with an insurance company. In 1894, after the publication of his first novelette, *Gefallen*, he gave up office work for the study of art and literature at the University of Munich. Then came a year in Rome, and from then on Thomas Mann devoted himself exclusively to writing. He was awarded the Nobel Prize in 1929.

He was only twenty-five when *Buddenbrooks*, his first major novel, was published. His second great work of fiction, *The Magic Mountain*, was issued in 1924. In 1926 the chance request of an artist for an introduction to a portfolio of Joseph drawings was the genesis of his tetralogy, *Joseph and His Brothers*, the first volume of which was published in German in 1933. In that same year Mann left Germany to settle for a time in Switzerland.

After several visits to the United States, he came to live temporarily in Princeton, New Jersey, where he lectured at the university. By that time he had published several volumes of essays. In 1940 his Goethe novel, *The Beloved Returns*, appeared.

In 1941 Mann moved to Pacific Palisades, California. It was there that he wrote *Doctor Faustus* and *The Holy Sinner*. In 1944 Thomas Mann became a citizen of the United States. Five years later he made a brief visit to Germany, his first contact with his native land in sixteen years. In 1952 he took up residence in Switzerland. There he wrote *Confessions of Felix Krull, Confidence Man*, the continuation of a fragmentary story that had been published more than thirty years earlier. He died in 1955 in his home at Kilchberg near Zurich.

PRINTER'S NOTE

This book was set on the Linotype in Janson, a recutting made direct from type cast in matrices made by Anton Janson some time between 1660 and 1687. This type is an excellent example of the influential and singularly sturdy Dutch types that prevailed in England prior to Caslon. It was from the Dutch types that Caslon developed his own incomparable designs.

The book was composed by The Plimpton Press, Norwood, Massachusetts, and printed and bound by The Kingsport Press, Kingsport, Tennessee. The typography and binding are based on designs by W. A. Dwiggins.